Free at Last

Free at Last

Bill Glass

Word Books, Publisher

Waco, Texas

ISBN 0–87680–489–X

Library of Congress card catalog number: 76–19532

"Free at last, free at last,
Thank God, Almighty, I'm free at last."
—Negro Spiritual

DEDICATION:
  Ed Green, J. T. Williams, Jerry Lundgrin,
  Pete Redmon, and Bob Cole. Five real
  friends who have unselfishly given of their
  time and means to make this ministry successful.

Contents

Preface

You may think that prisons are all dark hell holes of lasciviousness and depravity.

You may think that convicts who populate prisons are the dregs of society, the bog losers, the degenerates, the most despicable law breakers.

You may think there is little that can be done to change these people. If that's the way you feel, I can understand it. Up until four years ago I felt the same way.

You may ask, "If you really felt that way in the beginning, why did you go at all?" Only one reason that I can think of: Love. Mothers and fathers, brothers and sisters, wives and children, faithful friends of these inmates visit them because despite the prisoners' crimes they love them. But why would a stranger go to see them? Again, I can think of only one reason.

That is why I began visiting prisons four years ago—love. The love of Christ. Friends and associates of the Bill Glass Evangelistic Association came under conviction that we should be witnessing in prisons around the country. I hated the idea. Our ministry was in city-wide crusades. I resisted it. I didn't want to go, but when it became apparent that God wanted me there, I went.

I suppose I quit resisting one night shortly before going to bed when I read some old verses with new eyes. *For I was hungry and ye gave me no meat; I was thirsty and ye gave me no drink; I was a stranger, and ye took me not in; naked and ye clothed me not; sick, and in prison, and ye visited me not. Then shall they also answer him, saying, Lord, when saw we thee an hungred, or athirst or a stranger, or naked, or sick, or in prison, and did not minister unto thee? Then shall he answer them, saying, Verily, I say unto you, Inasmuch as ye did it not*

11

to one of the least of these, ye did it not unto me (Matt. 25:42–45).

This book is about the miraculous things that happened when I took those verses to heart.

BILL GLASS

Acknowledgments

Special appreciation to Fred Bauer for his inspirational encouragement, suggestions, and many editorial helps.

To Janie Andrus, my secretary, who typed and retyped the manuscript, always cheerful and encouraging in spite of long hours and hard work. It was more than just a job for her—it was a ministry.

To Gordon Heffern, whose prodding was used by God to begin this ministry.

To inmates in all prison crusades, whose openness and appreciation were the greatest encouragement to continue.

To dedicated prison counselors, who unselfishly counseled and worked with the inmates at their own expense of time and money.

To hundreds of committed chaplains and wardens, like Chaplain Bill Counselman and Wardens Ray Gray and Pete Perini.

To the Fellowship of Christian Athletes for the "sports clinic" idea.

To Bill Bright and Campus Crusade for the Four Spiritual Laws; to Billy Graham for the crusade idea, and good advance and better follow-up example.

To the many cities where we've done city-wide crusades, which have furnished us with hundreds of trained counselors.

To several people never or seldom mentioned in this book, but who have been involved in the overall success of this ministry: Board Chairman Garry Kinder; Crusade Directors Bill Carlson, Clyde Dupin, Dick Rohrer, and Dale Martin; last and

13

perhaps most important, my understanding wife, Mavis, and Mary Glass, Association office manager and author's mother.

It has occurred to me that though these crusades are totally unique, they are really only the outgrowth of my Christian background and exposure to the above mentioned Christian organizations. It is the way that all of these elements are put together that exemplifies God's unique leadership of this ministry!

"Nick the Greek" at Mansfield State Reformatory

Chapter One

Four years ago I reluctantly led a three-day crusade at the Ohio State Reformatory in Mansfield, Ohio. I say reluctantly, because I doubted that I had any business there. I doubted that I would be effective. I doubted that the inmates were really interested in hearing the Word of God or that they would respond to it.

The piece of paper I hold in my hand—a letter from a young inmate whom I came to know as "Nick the Greek"—is evidence of how wrong I was, of how far I had to come as a Christian, of how much God can use even less than totally obedient servants.

Let me quote from the letter and perhaps you'll begin to understand what I mean. The first part of it is a dramatic retelling of how the man got into the kind of trouble that resulted in a prison term; the second part is what happened when he found the missing element in his life—Jesus Christ.

Dear Bill:

I am from a Greek island called Khios (or Chios). I am from a big family; my mother and dad had sixteen kids. There are nine living now, five boys and four girls. I am seventh in line. We were raised very religious, to fear God and Christ. My mom and dad never really got along. He was a heavy drinker and a heavy gambler. Life in Greece seemed hard to us kids, but later I wished I had never known of America.

My mom raised us. She had a general store and we were always working. We never learned to play games. We had to go to school six days a week. Sundays, my brother Louie and I were in church helping the priest as altar boys. We didn't have electricity in the house, only in the store. On hot summer nights we would sit on our flat roof and hear my old grandma tell Bible stories. In our heads we knew about the Bible saints. When I was small, the immigration people caught up with my brother who had entered the U.S. illegally. They gave him a choice—fight with the American army in Korea or go back to Greece. He became an American citizen with many, many war medals. He sent for us. I was nine and a half years old at the time. Our prayers were answered. My brother owned a restaurant in Detroit and we stayed there six months before moving to Cleveland. I remember how happy I was when my oldest brother, George, spent $100 on Louie, Angelo, and myself for long pants and long-sleeved shirts.

But our troubles started in Cleveland. The first

day in school the kids jumped on us and tore our clothes. We didn't know English, so we had a tag card with our name and address. We felt bad because of the beatings—unwanted in America. We tried to tell the teacher what was happening, but the teacher didn't like us either. My mom and brother told us: "Don't talk back." We tried to explain that we didn't know how to talk back. In school, the teacher would find something wrong and make us stand in the back of the room. Louie and I tried to talk to the priest, but he said, "Don't act hard and you won't have any trouble." We got tired of the beatings and Louie said, "Let's fight back and kill a few of those stinking Americans." I always wanted to make friends, not enemies.

We had problems at home. Mom and dad decided to call it quits after thirty years. Dad would make us go out at night and shine shoes in bars. Dad always carried a few thousand dollars in his money belt. He would take our money and never give us even 25 cents for a movie.

As I remember, he gave mom $10 a week to buy food for eight people. I hated my father very much, but I was taught to respect him. Hate was filling my insides: hate for my father, hate for people in general, hate for God, hate for this country we came to. This was a phony world to us.

One day in English class the teacher cracked me over the head with two hard-backed dictionaries. I snatched the books from her and threw them out the window. I ran home and went to my room. The next day, Louie and I got beat up again. When we returned to school, we had clubs and chains. Wow! Were those kids surprised to see us fight back. We busted a few heads, girls included. We had turned into wild animals.

Day after day, Louie and I had to stay on our

knees in a corner of the principal's office. One time a
teacher hit me so hard he knocked me out. I burned
his car the next day. The kids were scared of us and
called us Louie and Nick the Greek. I remember the
day Louie beat up the strongest kid in school.

My mom didn't know about our running around
with a gang of kids. One father came to our house
asking mom to pay for the teeth Louie knocked out
of his son's mouth. Mom didn't understand and the
man got hostile. I took a baseball bat and busted him
in the face. We told the father we would burn his
house if he went to the police.

Mom was crying and she wanted us to go to
church and ask God's forgiveness. We loved mom,
but we didn't want forgiveness. About that time, we
started lying to her. Nobody in church knew we had
trouble. We were like angels at the altar. We kept
the masks on until we went home and changed into
our black shirts and pants and pointed shoes.

Now we were gang leaders—wine, beer, booze and
partying with the girls. Louie had been kicked out
of Thomas Edison School. He was a year and a half
older than me. I went to another school and the
teacher was nice to me. She taught me English from
kindergarten books. I finished the sixth grade with
honors. I started junior high school at Edison School
at 79th and Hough. Louie was going to the same
school. He made all the kids pay protection so they
wouldn't get beat up. Louie hit a gym teacher in the
face and was out of school again. Louie wound up in
a boy's industrial school.

My problems began again. Everyone wanted to
get even with me and came after me. I carried a
hatchet to school with me. I was fast with a knife
and with an ax or meat cleaver. Louie came back
from the industrial school, and no one could believe

the hate we had in us. Church was not our thing any more.

In 1959 and 1960 we were one of the biggest gangs in Cleveland. We ran a bakery out of business and bought the delivery trucks cheap. We rode the trucks all over Ohio meeting with other gangs.

I don't want you to think I was a tough guy. I was really scared. I didn't give the other guys the first chance. Our mom would doctor our wounds with tears in her eyes. I had my foot cut bad and I didn't tell her. I tried to doctor it myself. I finally couldn't stand the pain and stink. Mom took me to Mt. Sinai Hospital and the doctors said they would have to amputate. I can still hear her words, ". . . No cut, no cut." She took me home and nursed my leg well again.

My oldest brother, George, had moved to New York and Louie went there to help with the restaurant. I started cutting school. When I did go back, I would be drunk. We were getting bold ordering the teachers around.

The principal thought he would put a stop to this, but he got jumped by forty kids after school. He came back with his head in bandages like a Turk with a turban.

I constantly stayed in trouble with the police, but someone was always there to keep me from going to prison. My adult life was fast and painful. One day I would have lots of money, the next day little. All the things I hated about my father, I was doing.

Every time I would get into a big fix, I would cry out: "God, please help me out of this!" It was the only time I ever prayed. I would drink $25 to $30 a day in booze so I could go home and sleep.

One day I got into an argument with a guy over a pinball bet. I didn't want to start a fight in the place because I knew the owner. I asked the guy to come outside—I was going to shoot him. Right at the door he pulled out one of the biggest guns I ever saw. He pointed it in my face and pulled the trigger. The gun didn't go off. I sprang at him, thinking the gun was jammed. The next thing I knew, it went off. Blood gushed from my head like a geyser. The bullet grazed my head. The hospital wanted to help me, but I left. I started having sharp headaches. I had to do much drinking to kill the pain.

On my son's birthday, I was having a party. I was told of a big job for armed robbery. I left with my wife, my brother, another guy, and my wife's sister to get all this money. We got caught fifteen minutes after the robbery. Of the five, I was the only one sent up.

That was the old Nick. Then, he became a new creature in Christ. This is what he had to say about our visit to the prison:

I can't find no words in Greek or English to express how beautiful I feel inside since the crusade. My only books were sex books and comic books. I gave all of me to Christ and said to do whatever he pleased with me and lead me anywhere he wanted. Since then the Holy Spirit really started an overhaul on me. I am not scared to stand up for my Savior. When I was Nick the Greek, people were scared of me because of the evil I did. People don't fear me now. I have a new gang. This is the gang that spreads love and his word. Since you came with your team, the gang has gotten bigger and stronger in numbers. Even those that made fun of Nick are joining the gang for Christ. I will never forget my brother, Bill Glass, and all the brothers that came down with you. I thank God first and then I thank you for those blessings during the crusade and after the crusade.

Contact with people such as "Nick the Greek" and other prison inmates who found Christ during our early crusades helped me to see the potential harvest if dedicated Christians would just go into these institutions and allow God to use them. There is a great hunger there, I found. And there is something else there—something that preceded our humble efforts by years, decades, centuries. That something is the Holy Spirit at work on the minds and hearts of the people who have been closed off from society, but not from God.

One of the most unchristian things anyone can say is, "Those people in prisons are beyond help." That statement denies the power of Christ to change sinners. But I'm getting ahead of my story. Let me go back to the beginning of our prison ministry when I was dragging my feet like a spoiled child.

Bill Glass in NFL action against Green Bay Packers

Chapter Two

For me, the beginning of this story has Topeka, Kansas, as its setting. The date was June of 1969. After twelve years as a pro football player—one in Canada, four in Detroit, and seven in Cleveland—I was calling it quits. Hanging up my cleats to become a full-time evangelist.

While I was playing football I had attended Southwestern Theological Seminary in the off-season, and after I graduated in 1963, I conducted several crusades that were put together by Bill Carlson, a minister who came to me in 1966, offering his services as a director of crusades. It was as if Bill were heaven-sent, an answer to my prayers. Over the last three off-seasons—1967–1969—we had conducted city-wide crusades in many cities.

But now I'd come to the decision all athletes must reach—when to retire. My teammate, the great Jim Brown, had quit at the height of his career—and I admired him for stepping down before his career began sliding. I wanted to quit while I was ahead, too.

A minor injury the season before, when I cracked two ribs, had nudged me toward retirement. But the development of our city-wides was the clincher. In Evansville, Indiana, for example, we had attendance of over 13,000 some nights with many decisions for the Lord. It was the same in Memphis, Marietta, Georgia, and most everywhere we went. The Lord seemed to be saying, "Now!"

I had called a press conference in the Ramada Inn lobby. As I walked into the lobby I saw all of the cameras and lighting set up in one corner. There were many people from newspapers and television, including an old friend Watson (Waddy) Spoelstra from Detroit. We met when I was a rookie with the Detroit Lions, however the thing that jumps to the front of my memory didn't happen when I was a rookie. It was after I was an established pro.

One night after a speaking engagement my wife, Mavis, and I returned home dead tired. As we entered the house, the phone was ringing. When I picked it up, Waddy was on the other end. After some nervous small talk he got to the point. "You haven't heard from George Wilson (head coach at Detroit), have you?" Waddy said haltingly. "No," I answered. "I sure hate to be the bearer of bad news, but you've been traded to Cleveland," Waddy said. His voice was tearfully apologetic, as if he were responsible. It was characteristic of him. A warm and compassionate sportswriter for the *Detroit News,* he'd only become a Christian about five years earlier. It followed on the heels of his daughter's close brush with death. When she recovered, he had committed his life to Christ, and it was a dramatic change. He had been a real "hell-raiser" before. But now he was one of the most zealous Christians I knew. We were close, and I loved him dearly. When I got over my momentary shock (Mavis sat dumbfounded on the bed), I told Waddy, "All things work together for good to those who love the Lord." "That's right," he said perking up. "And you'll like the Browns. They're a great ball club, and you'll be able to play for the great Paul Brown."

Waddy and I met daily during my first training camp at Detroit for Bible study and prayer. I was a scared rookie coming into the Detroit Lion training camp under great pressure. I was their first draft choice. Bobby Lane and Tobin Rote were the quarterbacks. They made it really tough on me because I was the offensive center. The ball had to be snapped perfectly. They weren't too concerned about my making blocks; they just wanted the ball snapped right—which meant *their* way! Of course, the coaches were very concerned about my blocks. But during those rugged July-training-camp-days of that first season, Waddy had been a great source of strength to me. He seemed to think that I was helpful to him in his early Christian growth. When I first met him, he had been a Christian for about six months, but already he was spiritually mature. He has continued to grow even more since that time.

Now, eleven years later, he was at my side, encouraging me to make this new step of faith. My only other hurdle to clear was Mavis. I wanted her to be 100 percent in favor of my retiring. I didn't know how she'd react. She was accustomed to the life of a football wife and had grown to love it.

She had honestly told me only a few weeks before that she'd come to enjoy the yearly trip to Cleveland and the return to Texas after the season. She was tired of the constant moving back and forth once every six months, but she enjoyed the many wonderful experiences that surround pro ball. She'd grown, along with me, to enjoy the excitement of preparation all week long for an explosive two-and-a-half-hour period of head-on competition. She constantly gave me words of encouragement and prodding to be my best for the game coming up at week's end. She enjoyed being a veteran's wife. Some of the younger players' wives turned to her with problems. She had many opportunities to witness.

Mavis enjoyed the Sundays most. Sunday morning, she would get up early and get the children ready for church. I was never there on Sunday mornings. I was always down at the hotel with my teammates. The coaches felt the togetherness of the whole team spending Saturday night at the hotel was helpful. We had our team meetings early on Sunday morning. In the meantime, she would dress the children, and they would go to a nearby neighborhood church and hustle home as quickly as possible.

She joined friends that we had made there in Cleveland, or a player's wife, and go to the game along with our boys, who were eleven and nine, and Mindy was only five, so she would stay home with a baby-sitter.

Garry and Barbara Kinder usually joined Mavis at the games. They lived in Akron, and were two of our best friends. Garry was an enthusiastic backer of our entire ball club and spent a great deal of time in motivation discussions with me. It was his job to motivate forty or fifty life insurance salesmen in the agency he headed in Akron. So he was well-equipped to motivate me to do my best in a different field, but one that also needs motivation—football. He had been a quarterback for Illinois Wesleyan College and a college star in his own right. He still looked like a quarterback, about 5–11, in good condition and the most enthusiastic guy I've ever known. Garry once said to me, "You sure can tell Mavis was a cheerleader in high school. She never stops yelling at a game."

About the only thing that would sober her at a football game was an injury, and I knew that she worried to some degree about my getting hurt. She would never forget an exhibition game we were playing against Baltimore at Canton, Ohio, in 1966. The players' wives sat in the boxes almost at field level. There was no track on the field, so the boxes were very close to the playing area. She had never heard how a game sounded from close range. In the second deck at Cleveland's Lakefront Stadium, you can hear very little of the action on the field. She couldn't believe the noise of collision as players ran into each other, the close-up view of impact, and the grunt of pain. All this had really shook her up.

Her concern peaked when I got clobbered on a play by a little guard named John Sandusky. I had beaten my blocker and was going for the quarterback. Sandusky, seeing me out of the corner of his eye, pivoted, throwing his hands to the ground and in a long, arching kick, hit me in the side of the knee. I thought he had ruined my cartilage, or dislocated my knee. Sharp pain shot all over the knee-joint area. I fell to the ground like a sack of potatoes, reeling in pain and yelling in agony. Since Mavis was no more than 25 yards away, she heard all of this and was horrified. As it turned out, my knee was all right, and within three plays I was back in the game. However, this did make her think twice about my continuing to play. But, I did for several more years.

Most of my experiences in football were rewarding though —after my tough rookie year. But it wasn't always roses. Early, Mavis had had trouble acclamating. She was reared in Harlingen, Texas, near the Mexican border. So she was not used to the cold weather when I took her north for the first time. Her biggest problem was to stay warm at the games. She literally froze until one fan suggested that she get plastic bags and place them over her feet. That did help. However, I can still see her after many games with a red nose, her teeth chattering. Tears of joy if we won, or tears of hurt often clung to her chaffed cheeks if we lost. In many ways, I think she enjoyed the twelve years of competition as much as I.

Mavis got to know all the people that sat nearby at games. After they discovered it was dangerous to criticize her husband's team, they became great friends and would share sandwiches and hot drinks through the games. Mavis confided that when we first went into pro ball, she was frightened. She'd never lived in a big city, and our first stop, Detroit, was huge and frightening. Being the wife of a rookie, the veteran players' wives were on the cool side to her at first. Some of them drank heavily. We were teetotallers, which added a little strain.

Another problem was that she never had learned to drive in

a big city, so she often resorted to walking. One time, she was whistled down by a policeman for jaywalking. The officer stopped her and asked gruffly, "What in the world made you want to walk across the street in the middle of a block?" She replied, "I always walk across the street in the middle of a block in Texas." Then she broke into tears. "Well, what brings you way up here to the North, Honey?" he asked sympathetically. "My husband, Bill Glass, plays football with the Detroit Lions," she answered. He began to laugh, and several spectators gathered around. "Look, dear," he said, "I'm not going to give you a ticket this time, but remember you're not in Texas. You're in Detroit. In the big city, you've got to cross the street at the corners where the red lights are." Mavis, who was only twenty years old at the time, and looked several years younger, meekly went on her way. It wasn't long, however, before she developed a great deal more sophistication as the wife of a veteran, and was popular among players' wives. It was that position and those ties that would be severed by my retirement.

When I told her I was considering retirement, I waited for her reaction. I need not have been anxious.

"If you've prayed about it and you believe God wants you to leave football for the ministry, then that's what I want."

Now it was June of 1969, and I was standing in front of the cameras. It was tough getting the words out . . . I feared I would sound super pious if I said I was retiring to be an evangelist. And in fact, I was already functioning as one during the off-season. "I've had a long and happy career in football," I told reporters, "but twelve years is enough. The opportunities and needs are great! Outside of the Graham team, there are virtually no interdenominational evangelists who are using good advance and follow-up methods. We are gathering a team of real professionals, advance and follow-up people to help us," I explained. The press conference went well.

The decision proved positive in every respect. Over the next few months I'd never been busier or happier. The Lord blessed our ministry in many ways. In 1969, we held ten city-wides with several hundred thousand in total attendance and over 10,000 people made commitments to Christ.

In the next three years, there was a steady growth of staff and successful crusades. But I was settling into a rut, really pleased with the ministry. Then Gordon Heffern came to me with an unsettling suggestion that we begin a prison ministry. He'd been working with ex-cons in Akron, and had become convinced more needed to be done in this area.

Heffern had for many years been interested in a rehabilitation project. A non-profit organization, of which he was part, had been working with ex-cons when they got out of prison. Heffern and friends would get them jobs and work with them in their rehabilitation programs. Often, they had been disappointed. Many of the inmates would wind up back in prison again. He decided that the way to be more effective was to win them to faith in Christ first, while still in prison. Then they'd be more prepared to live a better life once they were released. That's when he began to encourage me to do prison crusades.

He was the president of Goodyear Bank in Akron at that time, and was willing to do everything possible to help us. His biggest hold on me was through Garry Kinder. Garry was not only one of my best friends, but also chairman of our board of directors of the Association. I got letters almost daily from Kinder, and it seemed that about half of them had some reference to Prison needs, problems, or opportunities.

I resisted. I'd had a long history of hang-ups about prison life. It all started during my senior year at Baylor University.

I had gone to Indianapolis with the Fellowship of Christian Athletes and thought I'd be speaking in schools and churches. But I ended up going with them to Indiana State Prison. One of the other program personalities was Otto Graham, the great Cleveland quarterback. We had walked up the long steps into the reception room. They virtually stripped us to make sure we weren't carrying any contraband into the prison. Then down the long corridors and out into the brilliant sunlight of the yard. It was well manicured. It should have been. They had a tremendous amount of labor there. But then we went into the large metal and concrete gym. The only wood in the place was in the floor. It was packed from top to bottom with inmates— thousands of them. The place stunk with the smell of their dirty uniforms and sweaty bodies. They really didn't want to hear us talk. They were relatively quiet as we talked sports, but when I mentioned my faith, they shuffled their feet and made noise to block me out. The acoustics were terrible anyway. The whole audience was a bad dream. I can still see Otto and me looking up four floors at all the men going into the cells. Hearing all the doors locked. They were in prison; locked up like wild animals.

I was determined right then that I would never come back to a prison again. It was stifling. This just wasn't a place for human beings.

As it was when I was trying to make my decision about retirement, I went to Mavis for her reaction. When I want to talk to her about important matters I take her to dinner. We have three children and sometimes it's tough to get a word in edge-wise at home. I had wanted to share with her the fact that we were going to do a three-day prison crusade in Ohio.

I started by skirting the issue. "You remember Gordon Heffern talking to me about the possibility of going to Marion State Penitentiary and conducting a prison crusade?"

"Seems like I remember you mentioning it," she replied. "Well, he has continued to push me to do this for a long time. I've been putting him off as long as I can."

As we sat in that Mexican restaurant, I thought, "Poor thing. She's been dragged all over this country during my pro career." In those twelve years, we moved twenty-four times. Every six months, we had made the long trip north to play pro football and back again for the off-seasons. We'd gone through seminary for the first six years in the off-seasons in Fort Worth. After graduation, we moved to Waco, Texas, where we spent the remaining six off-seasons that I played. We spent three years in Waco, after retirement from the game, but decided we had to get closer to the airport because of my constant traveling. So we moved to Dallas where there is a major airport and accessability to what had developed into a national ministry.

"Finally about a year ago, I agreed to go if all the conditions were right," I continued explaining to Mavis. "I really kinda hoped that something would happen and the door would close. However, all of the officials at this Ohio Penitentiary—the wardens, the chaplains and everybody, continue to be anxious for us to come. Today I got a letter from the Director of Prisons for the state of Ohio, and he is equally anxious to have us come."

"Won't that be a pretty tough audience?" she questioned. "Yes," I admitted, "but I'm certain they will be responsive to our message."

There was a real question in my mind, but I couldn't let her know it.

No one had ever tried it before. Who ever heard of a prison crusade? Those words almost contradicted each other. Prison means confined, closed, captive. Crusade means to me an openness to receive a whole new way of life through Christ. Most of these inmates couldn't be interested, I told myself. The majority, I'd guess, weren't sorry for their crimes, they were just sorry they got caught. Besides, a lot of friends were saying to me, "Don't waste your time. We coddle these criminals too much, anyway." "We're soft on them." "Put lawbreakers behind bars and throw away the key." "Bring back the death penalty."

There was no way we could work the prison ministry into our already over-crowded city-wide ministry. We had four full-time staff members, and they were all busy with our city-wide crusades. How could I break any of them free to help in preparation and follow-up for a prison program? I was so anxious that the city-wides answer the criticism that is so often heard of city-wide crusades, that they don't really have a lasting impact because there is no follow-up and no advance work. I was determined that they would have real integrity, with both advance preparation and follow-up work done thoroughly.

But they had started talking about a prison crusade about a year and a half before. I was always a sucker for planning something in the distant future. I could plan it for a year and a half from now, and it could be that for some reason it would fall through. The door would close. Maybe the prison officials would decide against it. At any rate, anything could happen in a year and a half. But the months sped by, and it was only four months until the prison crusade, that I began to get seriously involved in preparation for it. Staff members had been there a number of times and had worked on it.

I remember the first year I went to the Browns. A part of my contract negotiation with Paul Brown was to allow my family to come to the little town of Hiram, Ohio, where our training camp was conducted. Mavis and the children stayed there in an apartment during training camp. This was a concession not normally given to players. We had to live with our teammates in a dormitory of Hiram College. Brown compromised with me. "You'll still have to stay in the dorm," he had said, "but I can get the family an apartment nearby. You can see them every day at least for a little while." This was inconvenient for Mavis, but it did allow our family to stay together. Between the two-a-day workouts and all the team meetings, I would slip over to the apartment and spend time with the family. This had kept us together and made training camp more bearable. But we both dreaded my having to be on the road.

She repeated the question, "How much will you have to be away to do these prison crusades?" I hedged by saying, "Well, we'll have to wait and see. We may fall flat on our faces and quit after one try." I had thought that maybe the Board might protest when I first mentioned the prison proposal. "How can we go to a prison when there are so many people outside of prisons that we haven't reached?" I imagined them asking. I thought maybe one of them would insist on our not going until we were able to reach more people through city-wide crusades. But every single board member was positive about the idea. Still I was uneasy about going.

"About half of the inmates in Marion State Penitentiary are either black or brown, and most of them are from a ghetto. It's not going to be easy to talk to them." When I shared these reservations with Mavis, she suggested we delay for a while.

"Don't you think you'd be better off just sticking with the city-wide crusades for now?" she asked. "Well, maybe so, but like I said before, we're probably too far committed to this prison crusade to back out now," I replied. "Where are you going to get the money to do it?" she continued. "Doesn't the Association owe a lot of money?" "About $40,000," I admitted. She shook her head as if to say, "It sounds harebrained to me."

Her reservations were nothing compared to mine. We had planned to film the crusade for a television documentary. And now, I felt forced to do it, even though I knew it was going to be one of the toughest things I'd ever attempted.

But now I was being roped into it. I resented this. Everything in me rebelled against having to go to a prison. Maybe I was too straight for this kind of a ministry. "Certainly somewhere there must be Christians suited for this work, God," I prayed, but he didn't seem to have a very sympathetic ear. The prison date just moved closer. There was no way out.

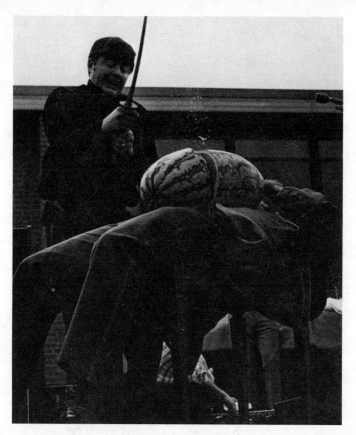

**Mike Crain chopping watermelon in two during
karate demonstration**

Chapter Three

I could feel the pulse beat in the veins running along the
exterior walls of my neck. While seated in the first car of a
caravan driving down the long, sterile entry road to the prison,
I told myself I was "leading the charge" on Marion State Penitentiary. Leading the charge wasn't new for me. I had done it
often in football. As defensive end for twelve years in the National Football League, I had descended upon my share of
helpless quarterbacks like a wild Banshee whooping and holler-
ing after a conquest. But that was during a game. Before a game
in the locker room, along the sidelines, I had choked on plenty

of cotton in the mouth and felt all those butterflies in the gut that come from nervous anticipation. Now the butterflies were back, as before we played Dallas in the divisional play-offs in 1968, only three years before. We had won against Dallas, but the "win" I now wanted was up ahead behind those prison walls, and I wasn't sure the team I had with me could do it. We'd had a great team against Dallas—Jim Houston, Jim Brown, Gary Collins, Paul Warfield, and many others.

Now, with the help of a few close advisers, I'd picked the best counselors from our city-wide crusades. So, here I was leading sixty men into a prison as if I knew what I was doing. What had I gotten them into? What had I gotten myself into?

I remember thinking, "I guess they're gonna go through with this thing." That's what one of my teammates used to say. It was just a bit of gallows humor, but I always thought to myself at the time, "That's the worst thing a guy could say." He almost implied that he didn't want to play. But it was his gut speaking. Somewhere back in his mind, there was the idea that he hated to go through with it, and maybe they'd call it off. It wasn't that he was afraid of getting hurt, it was just the pressure of the whole situation. Now, the same emotions were flooding my mind as if tapes were being replayed in my head, and most of them seemed negative.

I always felt anxious to play football, but this was different. There were so many unknowns. I was unprepared, and there was so much at stake. Sam Bender, my friend and co-worker, shared the front seat with me. The back seat was filled with chattering counselors. Sam hadn't said much since we left the motel. We could almost read each other's mind because we had been through the football wars together. He didn't play, but he had been a close buddy. I first met Sam when we were playing an exhibition game in Toledo, Ohio, in 1959. I was with Detroit at the time. Sportswriter Watson Spoelstra had told me of Sam Bender. "He's one of the most dynamic Christians I've ever met," Waddy had told me. He didn't exaggerate. After the game was over in Toledo, Sam met us in the dressing room. I knew from the first time I laid eyes on him that I would like him. He had a ready smile and quick wit. Waddy and I went over to his house—a beautiful home in one of Toledo's exclusive sections. However, he was one of the warmest people I'd ever gotten to know. He worked with his uncle in a tool and dye business in Toledo. Sam owned a large part of the business himself, and was one of the chief operating officers. This left him free to come to all of our games. A couple of years later I was traded to Cleveland. Our friendship grew and he became one of my best friends. In his mid-forties, with blond, curly hair and a sparkling personality, Sam was extremely popular as a speaker for our team chapel services. For me, he was a spiritual adviser. We talked, prayed, and suffered together through those years. He was an enthusiastic cheerleader in our victories, and a sympathetic friend in our defeats. Now he was a full-time member of our team. His business of thirty years had been liquidated and he could afford to live on the meager salary that the Association paid him. Sam was our new prison crusade director. When I say "new," it's the understatement of all time. No one had ever tried a prison crusade, and this was our first one. "You could be out of a job in a hurry," I'd joked with him.

We weren't alone, though, while driving up to the Marion institution. Sixty counselors from our city-wide crusades were with us. They were of little comfort, however. Each looked as if he was a sheep about to be sheared. Sure, each one had been well trained by the staff of our city-wides, but this was continents away from the warm music, friends, and the Christian atmosphere they'd known.

As we walked up to the prison gate I surveyed the chain link fence, thirty-feet high, stretching out a quarter of a mile in either direction. Barbed wire was rolled up on top. Behind that first fence was another of the same size, about ten yards away. There was a guardhouse at the entrance gate. Ganging up behind us were those overgrown Sunday school boys we called counselors. How I wished for a well-disciplined team of professionals, but all I had was a few sand lotters who had grown up in church, with their "praise the Lord" and "glory hallelujah" language. I was afraid they wouldn't have much identification with the inmates. In a situation such as this, one would need to be adaptable, cool, shrewd. They were none of these.

We told them to dress casually, and in a brief orientation session, we tried to coach them how best to communicate with the inmates. I said, "To the Jew you become a Jew; to the Greek as a Greek; to the wise as wise; to the . . ." But somehow I doubted them capable. One look at these guys and the inmates, I told myself, would say, "Oh, brother, here's another bunch of do-gooders, Lilies of the Valley Church, who've come to cram their brand of Christianity down our throats."

I comforted myself by saying that maybe the athletes would do better, but then I thought about unpredictable Paul Anderson, the world's strongest man. The *Guiness Book of World Records* gives him this title for lifting 6,250 pounds. He also won a gold medal in the 1956 Olympics. He'd be like a bull in a china closet if someone said anything to make him mad. I could just see the headlines describing a riot that resulted from Paul's impetuousness. In a fight, I am sure Anderson wouldn't be the one to get hurt, but a lot of inmates might get banged up and that would be the end of our prison crusades.

Karate expert Mike Crain could cause the same kind of mayhem. He does a thing where he chops a watermelon in two with a sword—while the melon rests on someone's stomach! What if an inmate got cut when Mike tried this? He does the trick often, but it's dangerous. "Dear Lord, don't let him miss."

Then I was startled out of my daydream by the slamming of the big steel gate behind us. Anyone who's heard that sound knows why people call prison "the slammer."

As we walked forward, George Joslin fell into stride alongside me. He must not have gotten the word on attire—his dark, pin-stripe suit right out of the "Untouchables." Elliot Ness where are you? George weighed 130 at the most, a skinny little dried-up man. I knew he was eighty years old, if he were a day. How in the world could Sam Bender be so crazy as to choose this kind of counselor? How could George possibly communicate to these hip-talking, young inmates? They were 50 percent black, I'd been told, and very anti-establishment. His best chance was silence, I thought, but he was a motormouth, a guy constantly spewing evangelical clichés.

"Sam," I complained, "you've got to sit on George, tell him to cool it. This isn't a Sunday school picnic he's going to."

By now we had crossed a hundred-yard ribbon of concrete, which was a sidewalk leading up to the administration building, and Warden Pete Perini was sticking out his hand as we came through the door. I didn't know much about him—only that he was a Roman Catholic who thought our coming might do some good, and that he had played middle linebacker for the Browns in the fifties. He'd retired about the time I joined the Lions. "Great to have you guys with us, Bill," he said smiling. There was a hungry genuineness in his voice that told me he was really glad to have us. "I have watched you for a long time with the Browns. It's really great of you to bring all these guys in here to help us out this weekend," he said. "Sometimes the inmates feel that no one cares about them." Just then the Catholic chaplain, Father Fury, appeared. A robust, jolly man, I could tell he was going to be a great help. Then along came a guy with a flat-top that was beginning to gray. Perini introduced him to me as Chaplain Ralph Wyle. He openly told me about how he had been praying for someone to come to the institution with a crusade ever since he'd gotten there ten years ago. I was concerned that this might turn Perini off. This may not be his type of language, I thought. However, everyone seemed to be so congenial in that group that it was comforting. We signed in, walked through a metal detector and through another huge barred door. Pete and I were leading the way. The chaplains and counselors and a few guards, fifty or sixty, trailed behind. We walked down a hallway for at least a hundred yards. The ceilings were twenty feet high. The hall was about a third as wide as a football field. Cellblocks were stretching out for fifty yards in both directions off the hall. Finally, at the end of the hallway, we went out into the sun-drenched prison yard and around the gym to the baseball and athletic fields. There were bleachers, and on the other side was the platform made of a trailer-truck bed. We nervously shook hands with a few inmates. They were unusually friendly. But they were the fifteen or twenty volunteers who were helping with the television, sound equipment, and other arrangements. As bells rang, the other inmates began to march out in great numbers from the cellblocks. Closely watched by guards, they filed into the stands. It wasn't compulsory, but most of them were coming because they heard of all the personalities who were going to be there.

Of the nine hundred inmates in the institution, I suppose seven or eight hundred of them were there that day. I sat uncomfortably on the platform beside Jim King and Cliff Ray of the Chicago Bulls. Cliff Ray is about 6–7—a great basketball player. Jim King is shorter and thinner, but still a hulk of a guy.

Our television director was Bob Kurtz, a former sportscaster from Chicago, who worked full time on our staff now and was acting as master of ceremonies. I remember hoping that it wasn't going to hurt Sam Bender's feelings since Bob was acting as emcee. "Sam's a selfless guy," I said to myself. "He'll understand." Kurtz got up and started gushing about how glad we were to be there. The inmates, sprawled out on the bleachers, were disbelieving. Some shouted funny lines (or what they thought to be funny lines) in response to everything Bob said. "Glad to see you here," Bob began. "I'm not glad to be here!" an inmate shouted back to the amusement of his friends. When he saw how he was bombing, Bob cut his spiel short and introduced Bob Harrison, our minister of music. Harrison was black with a big smile and bouncy style. I thought he would go over much better with the blacks, but they didn't like him much either. They must be color-blind, I thought. Giving up, he introduced the prison choir, which began singing "Christ for Me." Bob had rehearsed the choir the day before for a couple of hours, but they sang as if half asleep, mumbling words so that no one beyond the first row could hear them. To make matters worse, a big black dude in the bass section was badly off-key. Naturally, he was the only one projecting. One particularly sour note brought a big laugh from the audience. I had a feeling the choir could do better than it was, but their friends' jeering made them self-conscious. They were miserable, and so was I. They continued, but quieter and quieter until one would have thought we were at a funeral. Finally, near the end of the song, one inmate yelled, "Hey, Charlie! This ain't gonna do you any good with the parole board!" Laughter drowned out the final chorus.

"Now we're all gonna sing together," Harrison continued. He was brave even to keep trying. They wouldn't sing along with him, or even listen. Some of the counselors sang, but not much better than the inmates. It turned out to be three solos by our choir director, accompanied by a hundred mumbling hummers and 800 observers.

Then Kurtz was on his feet again introducing Cliff Ray of the Chicago Bulls. I thought to myself, "He's big, black, and tough-looking. They'll at least quiet down and listen to what *he* has to say." But no such luck. When he got up, they were a little better, but only for a few moments. Finally, floundering like a drowning swimmer, Cliff gave up. "See y'all tomorrow at the basketball clinic," he finished bravely. Then, to the applause he'd get for a missed free throw, he hurriedly sat down. We had planned to introduce Jim King, but I whispered to Kurtz, "You'd better forget Jim this time around. If Cliff didn't interest them, Jim and his white face won't." So, Kurtz simply pointed to Jim and said lamely, "Jim King will help Cliff Ray tomorrow in the basketball clinic." A single, un-enthusiastic "boo" greeted that news.

Then Harrison stood to do a solo, scheduled right before my talk. I've seen game people before, but this was downright masochistic. He had a good voice and did his number well, but never has one singer given so much effort for such little appreciation. I looked for an exit, but there was no way out. Maybe I could pretend illness. Pretend, heck! I was getting sicker by the minute. Finally, Harrison finished and Kurtz introduced me. I had told him that we should stick to the football introduction. I had asked him not to use any Christian-talk in my introduction at all. It was right to the point. "All-American,

All-Pro, defensive end of the Cleveland Browns, and the Detroit Lions, Bill Glass." I was walking up to the podium, my hands shaking. This was worse than any opening kickoff. "God, help me grab them," I prayed.

Hesitantly, I began with a football story:

> I'll tell you what I feel this evening. It's like the time I was rushing the quarterback coming in from the defensive right. Paul Wiggins, now head coach of the Kansas City Chiefs, was coming from the defensive left end. The quarterback was Charlie Johnson. Charlie weighed about 180 pounds. I weighed about 260. Paul Wiggins weighed about 250. The official was watching us two big brutes come from opposite sides, about to make mincemeat out of this little helpless, skinny, scrawny quarterback. Right at the last second, just before I clobbered Charlie from the blind side (one of the things defensive ends dream about), the official, who has a naturally protective attitude toward quarterbacks, yelled, "Watch out!" When he yelled the quarterback ducked. When he ducked, the other defensive end and I hit head-on. POW! Both of us just melted to the ground like characters in a Daffy Duck cartoon. The first thing I remember was this big official bending over me, peering down and saying, "Oh, Bill, I'm sorry." [To my surprise, the inmates were laughing.] I pulled him down to where he could hear me speak, because I couldn't speak above a whisper, and I whispered, "You know, you really shouldn't have done that." [Another laugh from the audience and their tone was, *I'll bet you really cussed him out.*] He apologized to me and to Paul Wiggins. That was the first and the last time I have ever had an official apologize to me for anything. There have been lots of times when I have been mad at officials. I thought they ripped us off. I was really mad. They cheated us!

But you know, there has never been a time when I wanted to play a game without officials.

Can you imagine what would happen in a game if there were no bounds, no rules, and no officials? A little back would run out of bounds and up into the stands to sit with the girls. We'd say, "What are you doin' up there?" He'd say, "Oh, I want to sit up here for a while." We'd reply, "Well, you're out of bounds." "What bounds?" "The official's gonna penalize you!" "What official?" "Well, at least give our ball back." "No, I like this ball. I'm gonna keep it a while." A game without bounds, rules, and officials would be ridiculous.

A groan or two erupted from the audience when I compared the game without officials, rules and bounds to a society without officials, rules and bounds. But surprisingly enough, it was small. They had laughed and they were now quiet and seemingly with me, to a degree. How long they'd stay with me, I didn't know. I followed with a few other football stories. I found their idea of humor different, they liked stories about me getting clobbered, and then got right into an illustration that I had grabbed for at the last minute before getting up to speak.

First base is an important base to go to in baseball. [I pointed to the baseball diamond directly behind me.] Wouldn't it be funny if a guy who was batting cut across the pitcher's mound and went to second base first? If he did, he'd be out. In the morning, we're going to have Bobby Richardson with us, an all-time great, all-star second baseman from the New York Yankees. He'll tell us a lot about baseball. But every one of you know that you've got to go to first base before you can get anywhere in baseball. But how do you get to first base? Well, first base in life is salvation. The way you get there may surprise you. It's not by being a good guy. We're not coming into this institution to tell you that you're bad guys and we're good guys, and that we want to make you bad guys good guys like us. That's the last thing I have to say. What we want to say is the truth, which is that everyone is a sinner. Every one of the counselors, the audience, the athletes, and surely me . . . we're all sinners. But we have found Someone to forgive us. That Someone is Jesus Christ. He can forgive you just like he did me. You can have a whole new start in life. The way you do it is to be a big enough man to bow your knees before your God and ask his forgiveness. But then you've got to go on to second base. Second base is relationship to other people. You can't ever really grow spiritually by yourself. Not only do you need to meet God at the first base of salvation, but you need to have friends who are also Christians and who want to help you. You meet them at second. Don't try to grow spiritually alone. You must have Christian friends.

On from there to the third base, which is service. You might say, "Are you trying to keep us out of trouble when we get out of this place?" And I'd say, "No." I couldn't care less about keeping you out of trouble. My concern is to give you something worthwhile to do with your life. Really happy people are the ones who have discovered the joy of service. They don't have time to get into trouble.

But what's home plate? It's heaven! [To my amazement, by this time they were really listening to me. I had their total attention. When I was through, I asked all the counselors to stand.] These men have come at their own expense from all over the country to share their faith. If you'd like to find a way that you can have all your sins forgiven and have eternal life, hang around. These guys will be glad to talk to you about it. Cliff Ray, Jim King, and myself will all be around here, and we'd like to get to know you.

Now, if you'd like, you can go back to your cell, but Warden Perini has assured me that if you'd like to stay and talk to us a while first, you can. We'll take about thirty minutes to talk to any of you guys that would like to stay. Now, don't forget, tomorrow we'll have all the athletic clinics: basketball at 9:00, football at 10:00, Mike Crain in judo and karate at 11:00, Bobby Richardson in baseball at 1:00, and Paul Anderson in weight lifting at 2:00. Don't miss any of the clinics tomorrow. You'll really enjoy them. See ya later!

That was the end of the service. To our amazement, at least forty inmates remained and talked to the counselors about their faith.

I had been watching Pete Perini during the whole program. He seemed appreciative. We had avoided a churchy atmosphere, but didn't apologize for our Christian message. We didn't slam them over the head with the Bible. He liked it, but I really wasn't as interested in Pete's liking it as I was the inmates' reception. I was anxious *not* to appear to be too big a buddy with Pete in front of the inmates. A lot of them didn't like the Establishment, and in a prison, nothing is more Establishment than a warden.

By dark, we were on our way out of the institution. Back in the motel we had a report session. The counselors were excited, though at first I wasn't sure whether they were happy because they had gotten out alive, or because they had had an opportunity to be of service. We had a little section in the restaurant to ourselves. The forty counselors and the sports clinic leaders were all sitting around talking. We shared one at a time. It had been a miraculous event how that service had turned from disorderly chaos to such an attentive crowd. When I concluded the evening with a brief talk, I tried to psyche the counselors up for the next day. Then we broke up. I hit the sack quickly once back in my room, as tired as I'd ever been. But I couldn't get to sleep. While tossing and turning in bed, some negative thoughts came to me. I had to honestly say that there were only forty out of 800 that were interested enough in what we had to say to remain behind to talk. But early in the service, I would have settled for a clean getaway!

Jim Redman of Redman Mobile Home Industries of Dallas had given our Evangelistic Association $25,000 to shoot a documentary of this prison crusade, and a television remote unit had come all the way from California to film it. Early in that service I had wished they weren't there. Our organization didn't need a documentary of a fiasco. It would only document and publicize our failure. As a fledgling organization, we didn't need any evidence of our inexperience. But at the end, the TV guys got some pretty good footage. Maybe the documentary could concentrate on the athletes. They would have exciting exhibitions. Even if the inmates weren't too responsive, we might get some good shots of our guys in action. Still, was I glad Jim Redman didn't come to Marion himself. He might have wanted his $25,000 back.

Saturday dawned a beautiful day in Ohio, and at 9:00 A.M. we entered the prison again. The fears of yesterday were soon immersed in the activity of the day. Cliff Ray and Jim King were super. The inmates crowded around by the hundreds to watch their basketball clinic. The playing surface was asphalt. The backboard was mounted on a telephone post, and the whole playing area was just beyond the baseball field where we had held the service the night before. First, Cliff and Jim put on a shooting exhibition, drawing ooh's and ah's from the inmates for their great accuracy. Then they chose inmates out of the audience to play with them, one-on-one and two-on-two. The two pros outmaneuvered the inmates just short of embarrassment. The inmates cheered wildly at every good play. They also laughed wildly when a con would foul up. In the chow line for lunch, a small black inmate said, "I'd shoot a long shot and Cliff Ray would pick it out of the air. He's like a tree. And that Jim King! Man, he's as quick as a cat."

The football clinic went well, too. I had given them some

pointers on the pass rush, and shown them some of my flashiest moves. I was dressed in a Browns' sweat suit—compliments of Art Modell, Cleveland owner, who had sent along his best wishes for success with the crusade. When he found out about our venture into the prisons he wrote me offering his help. I wrote back asking for a Browns' sweat suit to use in the exhibition.

Mike Crain conducted a judo and karate clinic at 11:00. The crowd had been excellent at the basketball and football clinics, but now it was even bigger. They had heard that Mike Crain was going to break 300 pounds of ice with his bare hands, chop a watermelon off an inmate's stomach with a sword, and teach self-defense techniques. Mike is an average-looking guy, short, black-haired, in his mid-thirties. He talks enthusiastically and fast. This day he wore a black suit—one of those judo- and karate-type uniforms with a cord around the waist. The inmates were most impressed when he smashed the 300-pound block of ice into two huge chunks with his bare hand, but they were even more interested in the watermelon exhibition.

He prepared for a long time, with the inmate growing increasingly nervous. The guy who held the melon on his stomach perspired profusely. The television cameras ground away while Crain performed. "I recently slipped and cut one victim . . . I mean volunteer," he joked. Then, suddenly, in one huge arcing stroke, he brought the sword down, cutting through all but about a quarter of an inch of the watermelon. He then told the inmate, "Don't move." This time he performed the same long-sweeping motion and got the other quarter of an inch. When he did, the watermelon sprayed all over the inmate's stomach. For an instant, the inmate thought he was cut. When he grabbed for his stomach, the other inmates laughed and applauded.

Then Mike asked an inmate, whom he had worked with just prior to the demonstration, to simulate attacking him with a knife. After disarming him, Mike handed two knives to an inmate standing behind him. He said, "Here, hold this for me." Unknown to Mike, the inmate to whom he handed the knife was a double-murderer with a knife. Needless to say, the inmates who knew that the guy was a lifer were more than slightly impressed with Mike's courage. Even Mike was impressed, so much so that he nearly had heart failure when someone told him about the guy's proneness with knives.

Mike concluded his demonstration by yelling over the P.A. system, "You guys come back tonight and I'll chop a watermelon on an inmate's stomach while blindfolded." They applauded heartily. No question, they'd be back.

At 2:00, Paul Anderson, the world's strongest man, got up. I was on pins and needles. He was especially loud and wild that day. I hoped he wouldn't make the inmates mad. Paul is an unbridled soul who has been known to lose his temper. About halfway through his demonstration, my worst fears came true. He drove a twenty-penny nail through a two-by-six with his bare hand. It stuck far out on the other side of the board. The inmates cheered and clapped. Then one inmate, like a spoiled kid, yelled, "Aw, it's balsam wood!" Paul Anderson exploded. Throwing the two-by-six at the inmate, he yelled, "Look at it for yourself!" The inmate jumped to one side to keep from being hit by the flying board, picked it up quickly, beat the board on the platform and shouted, "It's real!" The crowd thundered its approval. Paul Anderson was the hero.

That night, as he promised, Mike chopped the watermelon on the inmate's stomach while blindfolded. The crowd loved every minute of it. Bob Harrison didn't try to get the audience to sing. He just did a couple of solos before I spoke. They responded well to him. Then it was my turn. I tried to tell a number of funny stories because the inmates liked humor. But they didn't laugh at the same things other audiences do. Then I launched into the message, and they listened.

Right after the service I walked up on a potential riot. George Joslin was peering up at one of the most muscular men I have ever seen in my life. There he was—130 pounds soaking wet, gray-headed with tiny arms and legs, looking up at a man-mountain. With bulging biceps and triceps, huge chest stuffed into a T-shirt, arms crossed, his black face peered angrily down at puny George. The inmate was probably twenty-two, George was at least eighty. His flowered shirt-sleeves were flapping in the breeze around his thin little arms. He wasn't in a suit any more. "I just want to tell you how you can come to know Jesus," George said. The inmate said, "Shut up, old man." George persisted, "Young man, I don't want to make you mad." "Well, then, shut up," he said. George said, "I want you to know, young man, that you don't frighten me." The inmate bristled and said, "How would you like a crushed skull?" I thought to myself, he'd better shut up, or he's going to get killed. I started to intervene, but something held me back. "You know," George answered, "I think that's a good idea. I think you ought to crush my skull. The Bible says that if you were to crush my skull and kill me, I would go to heaven to be with the Lord." George closed his eyes as if to wait for his death. But then he opened his eyes and said, "One more thing I want you to know, I love you."

That was too much for Mr. Muscles. Suddenly, he broke out laughing. The next thing I knew they were deep in conversation. Before the day was out, he had accepted the Lord.

Bill Glass speaking to inmates at LaGrange Prison

Chapter Four

The television documentary on Marion turned out well, although the high-powered mobile unit that we had gotten from California did only a mediocre job. Their audio equipment was poor and the sound track turned out less than excellent, but it was usable.

We got Roger Staubach, quarterback of the Dallas Cowboys, to serve as master of ceremonies in the film and Bart Starr, then quarterback of the Green Bay Packers, to introduce me. The Marion crusade came during training camp so they couldn't be there in person, but they agreed to tape their parts to be dubbed in later.

The last day at Marion had gone well. On Sunday morning several counselors gave testimonies. A black musical group called the "McCary" performed a rock concert on Sunday afternoon. The inmates loved it. The beat was wild, but the lyrics carried a powerful Christian message. These youngsters—three young men and three young women—were for real and the inmates were impressed. Radiant smiles and bubbly personalities made their witness beautiful.

For the evening service we went inside the chapel for the first time. We had avoided the chapel purposely, thinking it was too "churchy." The inmates were much like people in our city-wides. It was much easier to get the non-Christians to baseball fields than to the chapel. But that Sunday night it didn't seem to matter much. They packed both the main floor and balcony of the chapel. There were many standing in the outside aisles and backed up against the walls. For one thing, it was being televised and they were anxious to see themselves on the monitors. Also, Staubach and Starr were going to appear on film. We had taped their parts earlier and would show them on the TV monitors to the prison audience. Almost every inmate was there. Man, was it hot! All those men in one chapel—900 packed into a room made for 500. But the whole thing went well, and we returned to Dallas triumphantly.

Two weeks later I was still savoring the good effect as I made my way through the heavy noon Dallas traffic. I was on my way to see Fred Smith and hated to be late. Fred was a busy man, and his time was valuable. Still, I knew he'd understand. He's like a father to me. We had met at a religious emphasis week back in my college days. It was the spring of 1957. Mavis and I had only recently married. A newly-selected All-American, I was asked to come and speak at William Jewel College in Missouri. I certainly wasn't in Fred's league when it came to speaking. He wowed them while I just kind of mumbled my way through. Yet, he was most complimentary about my talk.

From that time our friendship grew. I am always strengthened by his words of guidance, though he gives advice in a gentle, warm sort of way. I look forward to every moment with him because I am always inspired and helped by his words. At times when things are not going right, or my perspective becomes clouded, he levels with me and gets me back on track.

Charging down Lover's Lane, past Love Field (the old Dallas Airport), I whipped into the parking lot and quickly found a place. Then, I ran across the lot to the front door of the office building where Fred has a suite of offices. I went up the elevator to the seventh floor and down the corridor, straightening my tie and putting on my sport coat. I ran into Fred's office and up to his secretary and breathlessly puffed, "Hello, I'm Bill Glass and I have an appointment with Fred Smith." "Yes, he's expecting you, Mr. Glass," the secretary responded. "Just a moment." A few seconds later, the office door opened and Fred bounded out. He was about fifty-five years old, with distinguished gray around the temples, thinning at the hairline. He always gives me the feeling that he is about to laugh, probably because he smiles easily and often has something humorous to say. He always has a funny story or interesting anecdote to illustrate a point. Extremely well read, Fred had poor formal education, just barely making it through high school, but he's spent the last thirty-five years of his life making up for it. He once told me he reads about five to six hours a day. A top management consultant, he has counseled some of America's major corporations but now has settled down to being the brains behind two or three corporations in Dallas. Affluent, certainly; influential, positively; but not the least bit materialistic.

At a nearby restaurant Fred wanted to know about our first prison crusade. "How did it go, big Bill?"

"Well, it was a great experience!" I replied. "There were a lot of inmates who committed their lives to Christ and we came out with a pretty fair television special. I really felt the inmates were responsive; though they weren't at first. Even the ones who didn't make commitments were given plenty of food for thought. A lot of good seed was sown."

I went on to share the contents of a letter that I'd just received from Warden Pete Perini that morning. He had written that he wished we could take the crusade to every prison in America.

The prison psychologist told us that we had better rapport with the inmates in those three days than he'd had in ten years. I also showed him two letters that I'd received that morning from enthusiastic counselors, who were also board members. The first was from Art Svedberg from Cleveland. He said, "I was scared out of my wits. On several occasions I started to go up and sit with the inmates in the bleachers. I'd take a couple of steps in that direction but they looked so fierce that I hung back with my little group of Christian friends. Finally, I worked up the courage to go over and sit down with a couple of guys and tried to introduce myself to them. They eyed me with suspicion—I thought, 'Man, we've gotten this young organization into a mess by coming to a prison like this.' Amazing, how things changed in three days."

Then there was a letter from Dick Osborne. He said, "I had never seen such a tough audience. They were a bunch of animals. I thought they'd chew you up and spit you out. But as it turned out, it was the greatest experience of my whole life. Count me in on the prison ministry. I'll do anything I can to help. Forgive me for being a doubter."

As Fred got through reading the two letters, I told him, "Dick Osborne wasn't the only doubter. I was a big Doubting Thomas at the beginning of the crusade." I explained to Fred that the thing which impressed me most about the crusade was the inmates themselves. After we broke through that tough outer shell, they were like little children who followed us around. "When we showed them that we loved them, they were really with us. Hundreds of them came up and said to me, 'We can't thank you enough for sharing your time and bringing all these great athletes in here with you to this prison.' " I told Fred of the many letters I'd received from them.

In the typical Fred Smith way, he listened. That's his forte: really listening. Near the end of our luncheon, he made some pertinent comments. As always, they didn't apply directly to the prison ministry or to me. In fact, he was talking about something altogether different. He was talking about a group of people at a denominational headquarters in Nashville, Tennessee. "Now let me tell you about these pros in Nashville," he said. "They get together in a room and decide to have an impartial experience in a new and better way to approach group discussions, or whatever. What one authority described as an 'experimental syndrome' is set up. In other words, everybody in the room wants it to work so badly that they force it to work."

Obviously, Fred Smith wasn't saying that he felt we had done this at the prison crusade; however, he did drop this into the conversation. He's too diplomatic to say to me, "Watch it. You might have an experimental syndrome here." He just slipped the thought in with the obvious implication: think about the possibility.

I did think about it on the way home after our luncheon. Had we forced the success at Marion? We had the ideal prison, not the high-stone fences like the one I went to in Indianapolis with the Fellowship of Christian Athletes during my senior year at college. This prison wasn't anything like that. There were large open spaces, plenty of recreational yards, and only wire fences for security. Pete Perini was far from a heavy-handed warden. He was really open, interested in anything to help the inmates. Even the location of the prison was ideal. It was right in the middle of the state where I had played football. These inmates were well versed in my career with the Browns.

We had a star-studded program for our athletic clinics. Paul Anderson's demonstration was nothing short of amazing. Mike Crain's was, too. The football, baseball, and basketball clinics were super. Doll all of this up in the beautiful tinsel of television, and it could make for a rather artificial situation. Maybe we had set up an experimental syndrome in Marion, and then came charging back to Dallas like knights on white horses home from the wars. Fred Smith had stirred up a hornet's nest in my mind, one that buzzed for days to come.

Bob Kurtz, the man on our staff who was in charge of television, kept encouraging me to go to Denver to talk to a great philanthropist about our prison crusade ministry. Several people on our board of directors, like Garry and Jack Kinder, joined Bob in prodding me to go. Finally a date was arranged. They were sure the man would be interested in our prison ministry, as he does a great deal of work in prisons. Rather I should say, his money does.

In September of 1972, a few weeks after Marion, I flew to Denver enthusiastically anticipating receiving money to put the prison film on national television. I was accompanied by Watson Spoelstra and Sam Bender. We figured it was going to cost a quarter of a million dollars to air it on most of the major stations in the country. It was an hour long and would showcase our prison ministry. Bob Kurtz and this wealthy businessman met us at one of the television stations where Bob had arranged to audition the film. Our potential benefactor watched. We squirmed. There were some flaws in the footage, yet it was powerful stuff seeing lives changed.

When we were through looking at the special, I talked about the ministry for about ten or fifteen minutes, and then suggested the possibility of his giving us a quarter of a million dollars to put it on national television.

He hesitated a long while before finally commenting, "Well, young man, that's a lot of money. I don't know if I can justify spending it for something as unproven as your embryonic effort. Tell me. What is your recidivism rate?" I vaguely recalled hearing the word, and thought it had something to do with the percentage of the men who go back to prison after they have been released. My mind ran crazily in a lot of different directions and my tongue stumbled as I searched for the right answer. Instinctively, I knew that my reaction was pivotal. I squirmed back and forth in the swivel chair, but I couldn't hesitate any longer because he was watching me carefully. I decided that honesty was the best policy. "Well, sir," I said, "we really haven't had time enough to gather follow-up statistics because we've conducted only one of these prison crusades. We do have a follow-up team going back into the prison weekly. It's too early to tell what kind of continuing impact this ministry is going to have on the inmates." He was unimpressed. It was obvious in his eyes.

Finally, he said, "I'll tell you what I will do. I won't spend any money on this television special, but I will be glad to finance a study done on your crusades concerning your recidivism." With that, he climbed to his feet, bade us good-by and left the room. I was stunned.

In the cab on the way back to the airport, I sputtered my feelings. I was hurt! But more than being hurt, I was mad. He had turned us down flatly. His offer concerning recidivism was out of jealousy. He had been working in prisons for years and spent millions of dollars and hadn't seen nearly the results that we saw in three days. He was trying to prove to us that his work was long-lasting and ours was a fly-by-night thing. I really worked up an anger against Mr. Big and his foundation. Secretly, I knew the real problem was that I didn't know what our recidivism was. I didn't know what lasting impact this ministry would have on inmates. I was a "Johnny-come-lately," a young whippersnapper trying to jump into a field that this man had been in for years. He had spent millions working in institutions. I had spent little time or money in prisons, and suddenly, I had all the answers. I had to honestly admit to myself that I was more emotionally involved than I thought. I had been dragged by circumstances and the Lord into this prison thing, and for a long time resisted the whole idea, but in the cab that day I suddenly realized that I was in our prison crusades with my whole heart. If there was any question about going forward with the work it was answered there and then.

We had gone to Denver with a great enthusiasm and anticipation. I was fully expecting that the big man would say yes. But when he said no, it didn't discourage us. In fact, it made me that much more determined to prove to him—and to anyone else that might be interested—that this was a ministry that would have a lasting impact on the prisons of this country.

Maybe this was just a single-shot success, something we

couldn't do on a continuing basis. However, we were getting a lot of counselors and other people interested in our ministry. They were anxious for us to do other prison crusades, and that still, small voice kept pushing me on. The television special was being shown in a lot of markets already. We were getting public service time free!

A couple of days after I returned from Denver, I got a call from Dick Osborne. "I was really turned on to this prison ministry in Marion. I'm like the early disciples. I've been convinced against all my doubts. I was a real skeptic at first. Now I'm convinced. Now I want to do something. I'm sure I can raise the money for the prison work. My idea is to go to every owner in the National Football League and get a gift for this cause. They've got the money and there couldn't be a better place for it. Most important, they know you are for real. I'd like to go to Art Modell [owner of the Cleveland Browns]. We should go to him first because he'll give and then we can say to the others, 'Here's what the Browns did. We're sure you'll want to do the same.'" I had agreed, but wasn't optimistic.

My pessimism grew out of an experience of only three years before, during my last football season in 1968. Though it was in exhibition season, I was still unsigned. We were playing against the Los Angeles Rams the next day. Art was watching the workout at Hollywood High School, across the street from the Hollywood Roosevelt Hotel where we were staying in preparation for the game. "Bill, I'd like to see you in my suite immediately after workout," he said. "All right, Art, I'll see you," I said. I dressed quickly after workout, rather nervous about confronting Art. I had hassled with him before about contracts. We'd gotten along fairly well, but he was capable of being tough. Also, he was very committed to the youth movement he was conducting on our ball club. "We must get some younger players on this team," he had told me earlier. I was just starting my twelfth year in pro football and at thirty-three was one of the older players on the team.

On the twentieth floor of the Hollywood Roosevelt Hotel, I hesitated for a moment and then knocked on the door. Harold

Sibry, administrative assistant to Art Modell, greeted me. "Come on in, Bill," he said. Art was warm, but he soon got down to business.

"Now, I'm going to give you my offer," he said. "No matter what you do, I'm not going to budge from it." I gave him a noncommittal stare. Art sat forward in the overstuffed couch of the elegantly furnished suite. He was at home in the elegant setting. He had been an advertising executive in New York before buying the Browns, and he had a flare for being dramatic. "Bill," he said, "you can stand on top of this hotel and yell to the top of your voice, but I'm not going to budge an inch." As he said this, he jumped to his feet for emphasis. His eyes flashed and his little body quivered. I knew he meant it.

This was the picture that came to my mind when I was talking with Dick Osborne concerning the possibility of Art Modell's giving to our prison ministry. Dick assured me that he could get Art to give to our work. I responded, "Dick, it could be that you can, but don't ever underestimate Art. He can be a tough guy." I didn't share with Dick the background of my saying that, but I could hear his words ringing in my ears at that moment, "You can stand on the top of this hotel and yell to the top of your voice, but I'm not going to budge an inch."

Dick Osborne interrupted my thoughts by saying, "If you'll just get Jim Houston to introduce me to Art Modell, I'll carry the ball from there." "Jim will help us," I answered, "but that still may not be enough. Do you think Waddy ought to go in with you?" "Yes," Dick answered, "I think it would be good." "Well, I'll call Houston and ask him."

I was confident about calling Jim Houston because he's a great friend. He was our team captain and an all-pro. Art would be impressed with anyone Jim introduced to him.

I'll never forget a chapel service our team had just before a game with the Saints in New Orleans. Afterward, I walked up beside Jim, who was peering out the window of our hotel, and asked, "What do you think, Jim?"

"I think I need to become a Christian," he responded. "That chapel speaker made us all realize the importance of our spiritual commitment," I responded. I was very careful not to single him out, but he wouldn't allow me to be that easy on him. "But you don't understand," he persisted. "That chapel speaker made me realize that I'm not a Christian, and I need to be one. Sure, I'm a member of a church, but I need to know Jesus Christ as a Person." I said, "Would you let me show you how?" He said he'd like that. Up in my room, I carefully showed him in the Bible the verses that explained the steps one must take to be a Christian. Then, we both got on our knees and prayed. He was elated with his newly-found relationship to Christ.

After agreeing to let Osborne approach Modell concerning our prison ministry and arranging for Houston and Waddy to help, I forgot about it. A month elapsed. We were conducting a crusade in Lexington, Kentucky, with services being held in the University of Kentucky field house. One night after the service, Mavis got back to the room earlier than I. She normally isn't with me in a city-wide crusade, but this time she'd come up for the weekend. When I came in she met me at the door with a big smile on her beautiful face. (We'd been married sixteen years, and she gets better-looking as time passes. One of the things that attracted me to her was how readily she became excited. Just the least little gift or the most insignificant event could evoke a wonderful reaction from her.) I could tell the moment I walked into the room she was excited. I knew it must be something big.

"Sit down," she said. "Why?" "Sit down," she repeated. I did a little soldier march to a chair and sat down. She said, "I just got a call from Waddy and he says that Dick Osborne, Jim Houston, and he went to talk to Art Modell. Modell gave them $5,000 for the prison ministry." I could hardly believe my ears. Art and I had been friends while I was playing for him, or as friendly as a player and owner can be. But $5,000 was a lot of money! I got on the phone and called Waddy. He was so excited that all he could say was, "Praise the Lord! Praise the Lord! We got five big ones from Art for the prison work!" He was like a kid with a new toy. This was his first venture in fund raising. He had been successful. I encouraged and congratulated him, but he wanted to give all the credit to Dick Osborne and Jim Houston. "All I did was go along for the ride," he said. "Now, Bill," he continued, "please call Art and thank him."

Luckily, he was in. I said, "Art, I just heard that you gave our prison ministry $5,000. I want you to know that you are the greatest!"

He said if we were doing half as well as Jim, Dick, and Waddy said, he wanted to help.

"Art," I said, "it's the most exciting thing that I have ever gotten into. To see these inmates respond and to see their lives changed, it's really a fantastic thing!" Art replied, "I know it is. I'm proud of you, Bill. Though we don't see eye to eye on everything, you know that I believe in God."

Art is Jewish so I understood perfectly what he was saying. "I'll leave that work to your wife," I kidded. Art had married a Christian girl who played at one time in a TV soap opera. She had given up acting to marry Art. Art chuckled and said, "Yes, she believes in Christ."

Now we had the money—and I really had no excuse for not agreeing to more prison crusades. It was another example of putting out the fleece. All signs were go!

Bill Glass talking to inmate at Mansfield State
Reformatory

Chapter Five

Eight months later, in March of 1973, we walked into
Tehachapi State Penitentiary, fifty miles north of Bakersfield,
California, up in the mountains. We stopped briefly at the
motel where we met with counselors and special guests, and
then went on to the prison. Still further into the mountains
from the little town nearby, we came to a beautiful level valley
made more serene by a softly falling snow which turned it into
a wonderland. It was too breath-taking for a prison, but there
it was. There was no mistaking the chain link fence, thirty feet
high, with coiled barbed wire on the top. There was still the

63

clang of the heavy steel gate closing behind us. And as it had been at Marion, the same nervous counselors trailed along behind us as we went into the prison.

There was even a George Joslin in the group—at least he had the same kind of extroversive faith. As far as physical appearance, they were opposite numbers. This guy was named Sam Bigham (name changed)—and he was both big and a ham. Sam was from Fresno and weighed about 250 pounds and stood about 6–3. He was constantly laughing and talking. "Praise God! We're going to have a great time!" he would boom, rubbing his hands together like a used car salesman moving in on an easy mark. He was so loud it was embarrassing. I was certain he'd turn the inmates off; he certainly had that effect on me. "Brother Bill, Brother Bill, great to see ya!" he yelled. "You remember me, don't you?" I couldn't recall his name, but I did remember his face. Who could forget that face? I tried to be kind, but somebody had to tone him down or we would be in trouble.

By now we had cleared security and we were out in the yard walking down a long sidewalk toward the mess hall located on one side of a huge courtyard encircled by low buildings.

There on the sidewalk outside the prison dining room, we met several counselors. There was Bob Cole and Pete Redmon. Man, was I glad to see them! And good old George Joslin, still vibrant from the Marion triumph. Then there were some new ones who had been with us in our city-wide crusades in Bakersfield, Fresno, and Visalia. I didn't remember all of their names, but most of their faces were familiar.

"Let's spread out and have chow with the men," I encouraged. They took my suggestion and moved quickly to the inmates who were beginning to congregate for lunch. The line went comparatively fast, and I shook hands with and talked to as many inmates as I could without appearing like a politician. They were warm and friendly. The tables accommodated four each and I joined three blue-shirted men and exchanged where-are-you-froms and how-do-you-dos while trying to choke down the typically poor prison food. After dinner we went across the courtyard and into the all-purpose building. The room was used as a gym, theater, and all sorts of recreational activities. The chairs were arranged in a semicircle and we began our services that night with group singing.

John Westbrook, the first black football player in the history of Baylor University and the Southwest Conference, joined us for the first time as our prison musician. About twenty-two years old, he had attended my alma mater ten years after I had. John dabbled in pro football briefly, but was now working with the Fellowship of Christian Athletes on a full-time basis. He had a great voice and an even greater personality which coaxed participation out of a reluctant audience. He'd had a lot of experience at FCA conferences all over the country, where the athletes aren't usually strong singers. Soon he had most of the inmates singing, which I thought was amazing. Well, at least we're doing a lot better than we were at Marion at this same stage, I thought to myself.

When it was my turn to speak, I started by plugging the clinics the next day. The inmates seemed excited. When I began my talk, several of the inmates wandered out. Then a few minutes later, some of the same ones that wandered out wandered back in again. It was baffling until I remembered what Warden Perini had told me—that most inmates have to make frequent trips to the bathroom. I assumed this was because they drank a lot of coffee, and also because they were emotionally upset. Prison is enough to keep your entire system out of balance. I could certainly understand that. However, it made it a little difficult speaking to moving targets. Seldom was there a moment when there wasn't an inmate either leaving or coming back in again. In all, several hundred were in the activities building that night, which represented about half of the prison population. I hope we have better participation tomorrow in the athletic clinics, I remember thinking, and we did. Most all of the prison population turned out for our headliners.

Both McCoy McLemore in the basketball clinic and Alvin Dark in the baseball clinic were big hits. The inmates loved them both. The same was true for Paul Anderson and Mike

Crain, who did their usual great jobs. It was a little tougher here for the clinics than it had been in Marion because we had to conduct them in the medium-security section, and then over in the minimum-security unit. We had duplicate services and clinics in both places. Our counselors also were divided into two groups. But the inmates were appreciative and I was sure they'd turn out that evening for the service. The sports clinics serve as a great icebreaker for our evangelism that follows.

On our way out of prison that afternoon we were on an emotional high. The clinics had gone well, and the guys really dug the pros we had brought in. But something which happened as we prepared to leave for the afternoon stopped me short and reminded me of the purpose for which we'd come: to change lives, and most of the smiling inmates had lives which needed overhauling.

Bob Brennan, a friend of ours from Madison, Wisconsin, where we had been in a city-wide crusade only a month or two before, had come along. He was going to be a counselor and also conduct a track clinic. A highly successful head track coach while at the University of Wisconsin, Bob's teams won nine Big Ten championships in track during his tenure. He had only recently moved from coaching to the political arena in the city of Madison.

Bob was excited—about as excited as he was when Pat Matsdorf high jumped seven feet six and one-quarter inches to set a new world record under his coaching. He had made friends with one of the inmates, and as we were walking out of the institution, Bob turned to me and said, "Bill, I met a guy I want you to meet. What a guy. I can't for the life of me figure why he's in here. I spent the whole day with him. We played basketball, ate together in the mess hall, shared a lot of things, and became real friends. I feel as if I've known him all my life. I can't understand why they'd put a guy like him in the slammer." A guard walking nearby overheard our conversation and smirked. "Would you like to know why he's in here, Coach Brennan?" the guard asked. "Yeah, I really would," he replied. "Well, first he knocked a guy out. Then he poured gasoline all over him and burned him alive. That's all." Bob stood there in shock with his mouth open, unable to speak.

Most of the fifty counselors at Tehachapi were from the Bakersfield and Fresno area. One of them was Ed Green, whom I'd met during our city-wide crusade in Bakersfield. He was now serving on our board of directors. In fact, Ed was the chief catalyst for our being at Tehachapi. I'll never forget our first heart-to-heart talk. He'd asked to have breakfast with me one morning at Bakersfield. At this time, he asked what he could do to help. I told him about the Association's interest in prison crusades. When he asked if he could help, I responded, "Well, I sure know one thing. We need a lot of help. It could be that the Lord has led you to do precisely that." From that time on, Ed has been one of my closest friends, helping in every way— financially and spiritually as well. Every time I turned around, he was there trying to be of service. Head of a successful oil drilling business in Bakersfield, he was free to do a lot of things in our ministry. First, he came to some of the city-wide crusades, and then he got involved in the prison ministry.

He had first talked with the warden, Jerry Enomoto, and both chaplains at Tehachapi concerning a prison crusade. They had agreed to our coming largely because of Ed's enthusiasm. "What a dynamic guy Ed is," other counselors who met him for the first time kept telling me. I couldn't have agreed more.

Sam Bender had come out to Bakersfield and spent several days with Ed in the prison only a month or so before. Things had been well planned, and the results showed it. Ed and his son Gary were involved in everything from helping with expenses to furnishing a taxi service for us between Bakersfield and the prison. Now he was obviously pleased because all the work was paying off. Getting the opportunity to work with the inmates was one thing, making it count was another.

Most of the other counselors were from Fresno where we had been in two crusades, one in the beautiful coliseum and the other just south of the city at Visalia. Of course, there were a few counselors who had been in the Marion crusade. They

jokingly called themselves veterans. In truth, it was a more experienced team of counselors than we'd had at Marion. They
had all been well trained in the city-wide crusades and were
doing a good job talking to the inmates about the gospel. My
only real concern was Sam Bigham. He was the lone sour note.
Was he turning a lot of men off by his overly-aggressive, lapel-
grabbing approach?

That Saturday night in the sharing session, Sam Bender gave
a report on our follow-up work at Marion. He said, "Marion
might have the most serious Bible study group going in America, or the world. These guys come in huge numbers every
week, and then once a month our counselors spend Friday and
all day Saturday with them. The once-a-week sessions go at least
three hours. The inmates are filling out their *Introduction to
Christian Living* booklets and they answer the questions more
thoroughly than anyone I've ever seen. The counselors are en-
joying the follow-up sessions so much they are now talking
about making it a continuous thing." I interrupted to ask, "Sam,
what do you mean *continuous?*" He answered, "Just exactly
that. They want to keep going back, forever." "You mean
they're going to have a follow-up group go back every week
from now on?" I asked. Sam said, "Why not? There are fifty of
them. They can go in teams of two to four, and no one will
have to go more than once a month." "What kind of materials
are they going to use when they finish with our regular seven-
week follow-up program?" I asked. "They're talking about using
Campus Crusade materials and whatever else they can find," he
replied.

"Beautiful," I said. Without any coaching these counselors
had taken charge and figured out an in-depth follow-up that
exceeded anything I would have imagined. Now, I wished our
Denver philanthropist friend had been there. A continuous program. One without a cutoff date. I'd call that some kind of
follow-up.

Also, they were helping the inmates when they got out of
prison. Already several of the inmates had gotten out, according
to Sam, and were being helped by counselors to find jobs and

get oriented back into society. This is evangelism and social action working naturally, because the counselors love the inmates as a result of getting to know them.

I concluded that night's session by explaining to the counselors that we wanted four counselors' testimonies for the Sunday morning worship service. I suggested that it might be good for Bob Cole, who did such a great job at Marion, also to give his testimony in that Sunday morning service. Sam Bender would be good to wind it up, but we needed a couple of others. Pete Redmon could give a brief testimony and sing a solo, as he had done so beautifully in Marion. But would anyone else like to follow? Immediately, Sam Bigham said, "Man, I'd really like to do it." I tried diplomatically to encourage others to volunteer, but no one did. So I was forced to use Sam. I suggested that it might be best that we use different people in the minimum-security side. He was working on the medium side. I thought to myself, "That way, he will get to speak only once." I warned him in front of all the counselors of the importance of sticking to the five-minute time frame for counselors' testimonies. I feared he might drag on for twenty or thirty minutes and ruin the whole thing.

The next morning Bob Cole led off beautifully. He had a powerful impact upon the audience. Then Pete followed with the solo, singing "Ship Ahoy." I studied the inmates' faces as he sang.

Then it was Sam Bigham's turn to speak. He was nervous, hesitating for a long period, saying nothing. Some of the counselors wiggled nervously in their seats. The inmates scooted further down in their chairs as if to say, "What's wrong with this dude?" Finally, he began by saying:

> I want you guys to know that I am the sorriest, most good-for-nothing scoundrel that ever breathed a breath of life. For years, all I did was get myself into one mess and then another. I've been in and out of jail a hundred times. Every time I'd go into a bar, I'd tear it up and challenge every man there to a

fight. A lot of people accommodated me. [He said that while pointing to scars around his lips and cheeks. The scars were real. I hadn't noticed them until he said it.]

This was the first time we had ever had an ex-con give his testimony in a prison. In fact, I didn't even know he was an ex-con. The inmates were on the edges of their seats, listening with everything they had, hanging on to every word. So were all the counselors. All of us were amazed, because we thought he was just a man who'd been in church all his life. He continued:

Before I left home Friday morning, my wife grabbed me by the neck and hugged and kissed me and said, "Honey, Honey [his voice quivered and he began to sob], whatever you do, go tell those prisoners what a great change Jesus Christ can make. The first ten years of our married life was hell on earth. You kicked me around and cussed me out and treated the children terribly. We could hardly take it. [By now he was crying.] But since you've come to know the Lord, your life has totally changed. You're the greatest husband in the world, and I love you more than anything else on earth. What a great thing it would be if a lot of those inmates came to know Christ, too, and their families could have a great daddy like you."

I remember one day I grabbed a 38-caliber pistol and I was so filled with hate that I wanted to kill everybody I saw. I charged wildly into the street, jumped into my car and took off. I was blind with hatred. As I drove, I passed a church, and for some unknown reason, I went in. I went down to the altar and fell on my knees. "Help me," I prayed. God heard my prayer. Before I left that altar I had committed my life to Christ.

And, that, my friends, has made all the difference.

I sat there on the edge of my seat with tears in my eyes. After this stirring testimony I thought to myself, "This is the second time in two prison crusades that I have been proven terribly wrong. I thought George Joslin was the worst counselor possible. But he turned out to be one of the best. I thought Sam Bigham was a big buffoon, an obnoxious fool. He turned out to be the best witness ever. From now on out, Lord," I said to myself, "you'd better choose the counselors for these crusades. I'd probably pick out some smooth-talking, good-looking dude. You'd better pick 'em, Lord."

After the first service, I insisted that Sam Bigham follow us over to the medium-security unit and share that same testimony with the other half of the men. He did an equally good job there.

That Sunday afternoon we had the J. C. Power Outlet, and scored high marks with the audience. They had sung for us in our crusade in Visalia, a wildly-dressed, long-haired Christian rock group. The inmates loved them, too. Afterward, our fifty counselors went about talking to the inmates about their relationship with Christ. There were many commitments made.

Two counselors were talking to a guard. They asked, "Have we talked to every man in this prison, or are there some who are in maximum security?" "Yeah, there are some in the hole, but it wouldn't do you any good to talk to them."

"Why not?" they inquired.

"They're pretty bitter people," he replied.

However, after some persuasion, the guard agreed to let the two counselors go and speak with the men in maximum. When they arrived in the maximum-security section, the only way they could get in was to strip to their shorts. It was a rule to avoid any contraband getting in. The counselors were told that they had five minutes and five minutes only. Introducing themselves to an inmate, Jim Farrington (name changed), the two men sat on his bunk, one on each side of the convict.

One of the counselors said, pointing to his watch, "Look, we've got five minutes to talk to you about committing your life to Christ. Would you like to know how you can become a

Christian?" Farrington said, "Yes, I would." The counselors took the *Four Spiritual Laws*, the little booklet we use to share our faith, and began to go through it.

> Just as there are physical laws that govern the physical universe, so there are spiritual laws that govern your relationship with God. The first of these spiritual laws is: "God loves you and has a wonderful plan for your life." [Then the counselors shared a couple of verses of Scripture, John 3:16 and John 10:10, and went on to the second law.]
>
> Why is it that most people are not experiencing this abundant life? Well, that leads us to the second law, which is: "Because law number two says that man is sinful and is separated from God; thus he cannot know and experience God's love and plan for his life." [He read several verses concerning the sinfulness of man.] God is holy and man is sinful. This forms a great chasm. Man continues to try to reach God and the abundant life through his own efforts . . . good life, ethics, philosophy, but he can never make it.
>
> The third law gives us the answer to this dilemma. It says, "Jesus Christ is God's only provision for man's sin." Through him you can know and experience God's love and plan for your life. He died in our place and rose from the dead. He is the only way to bridge this gap between man and God. God has bridged the chasm which separates us from him by sending his Son, Jesus Christ, to die on a cross in our place. It is not enough to just know these three laws.
>
> You must also know the fourth law which says, "We must individually receive Jesus Christ as Lord and Savior, then we can know and experience God's love and plan for our lives." First, we must receive Christ; second, we must receive Christ through faith; third, we must receive Christ by personal invitation.

The Bible says in Revelation 3:20, "Behold, I stand at the door and knock. If anyone hears my voice and opens the door, I will come in to him." Receiving Christ involves turning to God from self, trusting Christ to come into our lives and forgive our sins, and make us what he wants us to be. It's not enough to have an intellectual ascent to his claims, or to have an emotional experience.

How can we receive Christ? Right now, through prayer. Simply pray a prayer. God knows your heart and is not concerned with the words but with the attitude of your heart. You might pray, "Lord Jesus, I need you. I open the door of my life and receive you as my Lord and Savior. Thank you for forgiving my sins, take control of the throne of my life. Make the kind of person out of me you want me to be."

"Does this prayer express the desire of your heart?" the counselors asked. "Yes," the inmate nodded his head. "If it does, pray this prayer right now, and Christ will come into your life, as he promised." To the amazement of both of the counselors, the inmate began to pray to the Lord, asking him to forgive him, and in his prayer he showed an understanding of the Four Spiritual Laws the counselors had just shared. "How do you know that Jesus Christ is in your life right now? Did you receive Christ into your life according to his promise in Revelation 3:20? Where is Christ right now in relationship to you?" the counselor asked.

The inmate said, "In my heart."

The counselor assured him, "Christ said that he would come into your life. Would he mislead you? On what authority do you know that God has answered your prayer? The trustworthiness of God himself and his word. The Bible promises eternal life to all those who will receive Christ."

The inmate had tears in his eyes and he said, "You know, my mother was here only seconds before you came. I refused to let her in to see me. I cussed her out. She often comes to visit me but I never allow her in. Would you do me a favor and run and catch her? I don't think she's had time to get out of the parking lot yet." The counselors agreed to do so.

They were quickly allowed out of the maximum security because the guard knew their mission. There were five other doors that they had to get through before they could get out of the prison. In each case, they explained that they were trying to catch the mother of Jim Farrington in maximum security. The guards were cooperative in letting them through relatively fast. They ran from the front gate to the parking lot, and as they were running they saw a woman pulling out of the lot. They flagged her down, panting for breath. "Ma'm, are you the mother of Jim Farrington?"

"Yes, I am," the woman replied, "why do you ask?" "Well, he wants to see you," the counselors said. "Oh, no, you must be mistaken. I was just up there and he refused to talk to me," the woman said tearfully.

"He's had a change of heart. He's committed his life to Christ. He begged us to come stop you and bring you back."

Parking her car, she followed the counselors back through the locked doors. The woman was disbelieving but finally she was persuaded to return to her son. They made their way to maximum security. There her son threw his arms around her and cried, "Mother, I want you to forgive me. I've treated you terribly, but today I've asked Christ to forgive me and come into my life." And that's the way the counselors left them—locked in each others arms.

Paul Anderson demonstrates his strength by lifting John Westbrook, Bill Glass, Jim Houston, and inmate

Chapter Six

So now we had two prison crusades under our belt. The success of the second one at Tehachapi drew even greater accolades than the first. Both prison officials and inmates wrote to thank our organization for sponsoring the weekend. In two attempts we had reached over six hundred known commitments for Christ. Counselors were hearing more results on revisits. The percentage of response in prisons was outstripping anything we'd ever seen in the city-wides.

Word was getting around between prisons. There is not only a grapevine within each individual prison, but between prisons.

The fact that we had had successful crusades in both Marion and Tehachapi was general knowledge throughout the country. For that reason, we began to get inquiries and invitations from many different states. The only thing that was slowing us down now was the money. We were discovering that it was costing us between seven and ten thousand dollars to conduct each crusade. The counselors paid their own travel and other expenses for the crusades, but we had to pay expenses for advance and follow-up work, literature, special guests' honorariums and expenses, sound systems, and musical groups. All of this was expensive. We could not afford to conduct many of these prison crusades because we were already going in the "red" on our city-wides. We owed around forty thousand dollars and were having difficulty meeting current expenses. The board began to pressure me to slow down on the prison ministry, at least until we were in a little better financial condition. That's when we came up with the prison gang idea. I wrote a letter to some friends of our ministry, which read like this:

> Prison crusades cost between seven and ten thousand dollars each. No state or federal money can be used for this outreach. We are limited in this ministry only by the ability to raise the needed funds. God has given us the answer, and we are excited about it. It's the "Prison Gang!" It's simple. The prison gang includes a thousand people who believe this ministry should continue, and who are willing to send ten dollars to our office each time we go into a prison.

The response was excellent. We simply send a notice about a prison crusade that is coming up to everybody on the prison gang list, and challenge them to give their ten dollars and pray earnestly for the success of the prison crusade. It has been gratifying to see how responsive the prison gang members have become. Early in our prison crusade ministry we had to depend upon big gifts from wealthy backers. However, to involve more people in our ministry seemed to be an intelligent move. If you have several hundred people who are giving and praying for each prison crusade, we reasoned, we will have a great deal more overall impact.

I thought I was conditioned not to be affected by the oppressive vibes which come from prisons, but I reacted as before when I arrived at the Ohio State Reformatory in Mansfield. It loomed cold and austere before me, not unlike an old Gothic castle. I wondered if there was a torture chamber hidden in some labyrinth behind its thick stone walls. There was no moat with alligators, but everything else about the place was just as frightening.

It was May 25, 1973, when we arrived. Spring, but the misty rain which fell on my face contained the chill of early April. Up a long set of steps we trudged—Sam Bender and me. Most of the counselors were already in the institution. Sam had come back to the motel to pick me up. They already had an afternoon demonstration with Mike Crain. A few of the late-arriving counselors joined us at the gate and they were just as nervous as ever. I didn't blame them. The place was really frightening. We were met in the reception room at the top of the steps by a cold-eyed guard. "Are you with that religious group that's supposed to be here?" he asked. I nodded. "The lieutenant in security sent me down to pick you men up." He motioned for us to follow him down a long, narrow hallway with ceilings thirty feet high. The passageway reminded me of the tunnel leading into the San Francisco Forty-Niners' stadium. This facility had the smell of a damp cellar. Nothing like Marion or Tehachapi, it reminded me more of the Indiana prison I'd visited during my college days. If you can remember the Edward G. Robinson gangster movies with their prison scenes, you can picture the Mansfield prison.

"Sam, this guy doesn't know what's going on. What happened to our publicity?" I asked.

"Bill, there are posters plastered all over this place. These guards are just spaced out," he answered. "I promise you all the inmates know about our coming and they'll show up." We were interrupted by our escort guard: "You know," he drawled, "they built this place back around the turn of the century."

"Which century?" I dead-panned. He didn't laugh. They seldom do. Prisons are sad places. A joke has to be a knee-slapper to get a laugh in prison.

Finally we went up a long flight of stairs to a big steel door with a peephole in it. The guard with us gave the nod to his colleague on the other side of the door and it automatically opened. We were now in a cage. On the other side of the cage were visitors, who had come to see their time-serving husbands, sweethearts, sons, friends. It was a rather large room, filled with bus station-type benches. I thought to myself how horrible it would be to have to visit your loved one in a place like this. Even worse, how horrible to be in a place like this and how embarrassing to have your children see you in this setting! There was absolutely no privacy in the room. It was jammed with visitors and inmates. Some were busy embracing wives or girl friends, oblivious to others around them. Children were playing in the room; one father was trying to comfort his small son who was crying over a broken toy.

Another was sitting quietly, staring off in space. He seemed to have run out of something to say to his family. He looked bored by their visit. The scene reminded me of something an inmate told me at Marion: "Prison routine is so boring it is nauseating. I'm careful to never discuss it with people who visit me. It's too depressing. Any trivia from the outside world is refreshing."

The mannerisms in the visitors' room were all different, yet the same—languid, passive, unresponsive. Their body language spoke volumes. Their looks in my direction made it easy for me to read their minds. "Well, what are you looking at us for? We aren't embarrassed that we have someone in prison," one girl's eyes said. A young black adult clenched his teeth and glared at me as if to say, "I'd like to hit you in the mouth."

An overly-protective, well-dressed, middle-aged white mother's raised eyebrows expressed disdain. An apologetic, heavyset father's resigned frown seemed to say, "It's not my fault that my son is in here. It's society's fault."

After leaving the visitors' room we entered a gymnasium-type room. It was at least six or seven stories high. The giant dirty-gray stones that we had seen on the outside were just as ugly on the inside. The solid wall was interrupted only by narrow steel-barred windows running from floor to ceiling. What little sunlight there was on that overcast day peeked through the windows in eerie shafts of light that reflected off the floor. Six stories of cages stacked right on top of each other, I thought as I craned my neck looking up at them. Each cell was about ten feet long and five feet wide. The ceilings within the cages were only about seven feet high. The doors allowing entrance into the cells were about half the size of the front wall of the cage. All the doors could be opened and closed by cranking one huge lever at the end of each line of cells. The cells were rimmed with little catwalks. As I stood gawking, the guard said dryly, "That's the largest cellblock in the world. There are fifty cells on each side. That totals six hundred cells, two men to a cell or twelve hundred inmates in one cellblock."

The odor of the place hit me in the face when I came through the door. It's the odor common to most prisons I've visited . . . sweat, tobacco, and some sort of acrid disinfectant they use to try to kill the smell. The sound was familiar. The noise of men's feet scraping on the concrete, the clanging of steel and the constant beat of the junglelike music that was played so loudly it hurt my ears. Again, I had the feeling of what a horrible thing it would be to be locked up in such a dehumanizing place. No way to escape the smell or the sound or the oppressive closed-in feeling. Or to be able to stand out in the open beauty of God's nature. Or to escape to some kind of lonely hillside where one could listen to the beauty of silence. But those are taken-for-granted pleasures convicts give up when they are sentenced to prison.

How hopeless. Nothing to look forward to day after day after unending day. Outside, in the yard, the sun was trying to peek through the clouds. It wasn't very cold, but I felt chilled—chilled by the whole downbeat quality of prison life.

We walked down a long sidewalk around the infirmary building and the gymnasium and into a cove. The cove was created by the gym on one side and a huge factory on the other. They make shoes in the factory, I was told. Everybody's shoes looked alike. In prison they don't ask if you like them fancy or plain.

The back wall of the cove was the outside wall of the prison. Here, the huge stones were covered with stuccolike concrete that went straight up for thirty or forty feet. At the top of the wall was a gun tower with a guard standing in it peering down at us. A semicircle of bleachers arced around two trailer truck beds which were parked side by side to form our platform. There were three rows of seats for the choir on the back half of the platform. The other half of the platform was left for us to do our demonstrations and for me to speak from. There was a crudely-built set of steps on one side of the platform. This was the best physical setup we'd ever had in a prison. The semicircle was full of folding chairs, which made the inmates very close to me. Even the ones that were the farthest away in the bleachers were still no more than seventy-five feet away. Then they began to file out into the yard. The guards marched them out by wings. Each wing had a guard, and they filed out in long lines with the guard flanking them. The inmates, about sixteen hundred in all, sat in the folding chairs and in the bleachers. There were about eighteen hundred young men jailed at Mansfield between the ages of sixteen and twenty-six, so all but a couple of hundred turned out. The place was jammed, which made me feel good, but then I began to look around at the faces. They seemed to be a mix between hostile and apathetic. Not having anything better to do, the inmates had come to see a show. It wasn't compulsory. When I took my place on the platform, the choir began to sing—very loudly. I thought to myself, "This is a better choir than the one we had at Marion. Maybe it was a good sign, but here they're singing at the top of their voices." Still, the audience wasn't appreciative and they catcalled throughout the number.

As we sat on the overcrowded platform, Sam whispered some unpleasant details of the afternoon clinic. "They really chewed Mike Crain up this afternoon. It was a complete disaster." Mike needs complete concentration to do his act, and according to Sam, the inmates yelled and screamed the whole time he tried to perform. He lost his concentration and when he hit the ice, nothing happened. The inmates laughed and made fun of him. Later in the program, an inmate accidentally kicked the ice with his toe and when he did, it fell apart. More laughs. Obviously, Mike had broken the ice with his hand and the kick from the inmate had just finished the job, but the inmates jumped on it right away. "Fake! Fake! Fake!" they yelled. Mike struggled through his program, but was ineffective.

Now they were taking up where they left off in the afternoon. They were making it really tough on the choir. These were their buddies and they knew how to razz them. The committed Christians ignored the yelling inmates, but I could tell it was really getting to some of them. Still, they kept singing. I felt proud to have a group like this behind me, so to show my support, I began to sing with them. Some of the inmates in the audience joined in. The counselors, who were scattered in the audience, saw my strategy and they added their voices. But about that time, the choir finished and John Westbrook tried to say a few words of introduction.

Then suddenly in came the homosexuals. There were about fifteen of them. The first one in the line was a black inmate who had oversized hair curlers in his hair. He was wiggling his hips from side to side, imitating a girl as he led the group in. Behind him were the rest, each one appearing to be more feminine than the one before. The last man in the line was a white, who swung his hips more exaggeratedly than any girl I've ever seen. A guard later told me, "They're sure they are women. They constantly chide us because we keep them in a male institution. 'Don't you know we are women? Why do you have us in a men's prison?'" The inmates responded with whistling and obscenities. The reason they came in late was because they were kept separate from the others. I was told if they weren't segregated, the other inmates would rape or kill them.

Naturally, their entrance disrupted the service, but John Westbrook bravely continued. Mike Crain gave a brief demonstration. He was a little more effective and successful in this demonstration than he had been in the afternoon, but they were impolite. Bob Anderson, who is in charge of sound and plays the organ and piano, was sitting to my left. I poked him and said, "Keep the sound turned up high. I'm gonna have to out yell them." Crain introduced me, and I got up to speak. I decided I would just concentrate on what I was saying, and forget them. I was glad I was familiar with my material. These were supposed to be sixteen hundred of Ohio's worst young men, and they were living up to their reputation.

I decided I would just pick out some of the ones that were the most interested in what was going on, and speak to them, ignoring the ones that weren't interested. To my surprise, as I began to look carefully into the eyes of the audience, they were listening. They didn't want the other inmates to know they were listening, but they were! Except for those very few, the audience was with me. It was hard to concentrate on the ones that were listening, because the ones who weren't were so vocal. Every statement I made, they would respond. "Hey, man, we don't need no sermon. We need a way out of this hole!" one inmate yelled. "Yeah, man," another picked it up, "why don't you talk to the parole board?" "Hey, man, Pittsburgh's our team. We don't like the Browns," tossed another.

I knew what it was to have heckling. There had been times when I'd been booed. Not personally, but as a team. I guess it hurt Mavis more than it hurt me. The first time it happened was in Detroit. We had won the championship the year before, but had had a miserable season in 1958. The next year, 1959, was even worse, and the fans began to boo. There were times after the game that Mavis would be in tears. However, it wasn't until 1966 that I saw the effects of personal booing. Mavis sat next to Joan Ryan, the wife of our quarterback in Cleveland. Seldom did they boo the team as a whole. It was usually one particular player. The player they both cheered and booed was the quarterback. Frank Ryan was my roommate, so it was natural for Joan and Mavis to sit together at the games. When Frank played poorly, the crowd would boo, and Joan was crushed. She often cried, and on occasion lost her cool and yelled back at the rowdy fans. Sometimes the fans would simply retort, "Look, lady, I paid my way into this place. I can say what I want to say." Mavis sympathized with Joan.

I remember Bill Wade, quarterback of the Chicago Bears, talking about the "down" season he had after leading the Bears to the championship in 1963. Late in that disastrously bad year, Wade got clobbered by a wildly-charging defensive lineman of the Detroit Lions by the name of Alex Karris. Karris caught him from the blind side and knocked Wade unconscious. "It was terribly discouraging to be booed when I did poorly," Wade said, "but the thing that caused me to retire at the end of the 1964 season was when I regained consciousness I heard the fans cheering. I couldn't understand why home fans were cheering, and then it slowly dawned on me that they were cheering because I'd gotten hurt. That was too much to take. I decided to hang up my cleats."

I had never known what it was to be booed individually. I had been booed as part of a losing team, but that was a little different from being singled out. Here I was, on this rather small stage, surrounded by inmates, and every word I was saying was being picked apart by the hecklers. Now, I knew how Ryan and Wade felt.

Even though most of them were listening, I still felt the service was a failure. After the service was over, however, an inmate called Nick the Greek, a Christian leader in the prison, came up and said, "Don't get discouraged, man. Most of the guys were listening. It was just a few organized troublemakers that were making all the noise." I wanted to believe him but I wasn't sure.

It looked like our negative experience early in that first service at Marion would have been enough to prepare me for what was happening here. But it wasn't. You can't ever get ready for this kind of treatment.

Right after the service Pete Redmon followed an inmate up on one of the ranges (catwalks that encircled the cells). Pete, who has worked in all of our crusades as a counselor, said, "I thought maybe if I could talk to him, he'd be quiet so others could hear. He was the loudest of the hecklers."

The man Pete had zeroed in on wore a beanie—an orange beanie—and was a muscular, but rather short, black inmate. He screamed and yelled at the top of his voice, and encouraged his followers to do the same.

Here's how Pete tells the story:

> I was working my way closer to the orange beanie as it bobbed up and down in front of me in the crowd of inmates as they were moving back to their cells for "count." [They are counted in their cells twice daily.] As I got closer, I heard the man boastfully say, "I'd sure like to talk to one of those crusaders!" The way he said *crusaders* spoke volumes about his disgust for us. I was surprised at myself, but I shot back at the inmate with, "I'll be glad to talk to you." The inmate turned and looked at me equally surprised, but he replied, "Okay, come on." We went into his cell nearby, and almost immediately, all the doors were locked on that line of cells. I was locked in with him. The 5-by-10-foot room seemed even smaller. The walls were covered with *Playboy* centerfolds showing naked women. Music blared from the cell next door, just six inches away.
>
> "What's your name?" I asked. "Lefty Dog," he replied. "Why do they call you that? Don't you have a real name?" "Nope, just Lefty Dog. I'm just a left out dog. Nobody cares about me. I'm stuck off here in this hole, totally *left out!* It's been that way all my life!" he replied. Lefty Dog's eyes flashed with defiance. For an hour and a half, Lefty ranted about all the injustices he had suffered. He was full of hatred. "You are just a bunch of fat cats. You're paid by the state. You're trying to cram your white man's religion down our throats." I explained that all the

counselors paid their own way. The Association pays for expenses like motels and meals, but the state pays nothing. I also pointed out that we had several black special guests and counselors. He dismissed them as token and Uncle Toms. After three hours, I left feeling I'd made some headway, but when I told one of the Christian inmates, he said I was wasting my time. "He's one of the most vicious guys in this place. He'll be the last guy here to become a Christian," the man said of Lefty Dog. Still I was determined to return and that night I asked the Holy Spirit to touch him.

The next day, another counselor was locked up in the cell with Lefty Dog. You shouldn't take being locked in a cell with an inmate too lightly. It was one of the first times it had been done in the history of the institution. After the second session with the other counselor, Lefty Dog had quit yelling and cussing as much, but still he was resistant to our message. I sadly concluded that the person who told me that Lefty Dog would not accept Christ was right.

Immediately after the service I was walking the ranges thinking that maybe I could get the feel of the institution better by moving around and getting closer to the inmates. Some of them sneered as I passed by, but most of them were pretty friendly on an individual basis. They were all locked in their cells now, and stopping at almost every cell, I introduced myself and talked briefly. Sometimes, the inmates wanted to talk longer. Many of them wanted their pictures snapped with me. Ron Kuntz, a United Press International photographer, who was walking with me obliged.

We had become close friends during my Cleveland years. He was at all the games and most of the practices, snapping photos. He was a sincere Christian. The players ribbed him a lot but they liked him. So did I. Ron is so small that he could walk untouched under most defensive linemen's armpits, which may explain his prowess at being so often in the right spot taking pictures from every angle. If ever he thought he irritated a player, he'd give him an apologetic, sheepish grin. Rather than getting mad, everyone would laugh at him. If they crowded him, he'd witness to them. I had a terribly busy schedule, but he was always talking me into coming and speaking to his church or to some group he was interested in. When I retired, we sort of lost touch except on occasional Cleveland trips, but when he heard about the prison ministry, he turned up offering his help.

Watson Spoelstra appointed Ron to be the crusade photographer. "We got the worst pictures in the world, Bill," Waddy complained to me one time following a city-wide, "and one of our best pals is an award-winning photographer. We must get Kuntz." We did just that. At prison crusades, Ron takes a few pictures and then witnesses a while. Sometimes he gets so involved in trying to work with the inmates spiritually that he forgets to take pictures. But he knows which is most important —and we also have gotten some great shots.

But in Mansfield, the picture-taking really helped us get close to the inmates. They would say, "Hey, man, take my picture. Here's my name and number. Send me a copy." Kuntz would oblige. I wondered why an inmate would want a picture of me when he was on the other side of the bars, but they all did. It was a great icebreaker. We did that for hundreds of them that night. They all really seemed appreciative. Then I began to witness to an inmate who wanted to know how to become a Christian. As I talked with him, I noticed that Ron was talking intently with the man in the next cell. When I came by Ron had the *Four Spiritual Laws* out, explaining how to become a Christian. A few minutes later when I came back to see what was keeping Ron, the inmate told me, "As I saw you coming down and stopping from cell to cell, taking pictures and talking with everybody, I thought to myself, 'I'll talk to that photographer. I'm sure he won't be a Christian like those other Jesus-freaks, and I can talk to him about photography.' I love photography, but instead, I committed my life to Christ." There was a smile on the man's face that couldn't be contained by bars. His joy was that full.

The love that develops between counselors and cons is another evidence of the power of the Holy Spirit's ability to touch hearts and change them. Otherwise, those widely different personalities would never hook up.

We went back to the motel for dinner and as soon as we finished eating we began to share experiences from the day. There were about forty counselors and each one had his own special incident to report. There was a very optimistic mood in the room. Bob Kane of Findlay, Ohio, reported:

> Well, there was lots of noise going on, but we've got opportunities to witness. Jerry Cramer and I traveled to Mansfield together. While driving here, Jerry told me of a woman where he worked who has a son in this prison. She asked Jerry if he would talk to him. Jerry told me that he felt as though God would lead us to Sam Barnes [not his real name]. We took our seats during the first session and some inmates sat in front of us. We talked for a while. They asked where we were from and we told them Findlay. One boy said, "I'm from that area. My name is Sam Barnes."

> Another counselor said: I know you're not gonna believe this, but several people asked me to talk to a young man from my hometown. I introduced myself to the inmate next to me and asked his name. It was the guy I was supposed to look up!

> Ron Kuntz stood to say: I have covered riots where blacks and whites were at each other's throats, killing and harming one another. The thing that stands out in my mind about the prison crusade was last night when counselors shared with each other. As I looked about the room, I noticed blacks and whites together, bound in true love because of Christ. It brought tears

to my eyes. To me, this will stand out above everything else, for I've seen only bitterness and hatred
while covering stories of riots.

I concluded the whole evening by saying: It's
really difficult to talk above all that yelling and
screaming. However, it's encouraging to know that so
many of you are being used by the Lord in personal
witness. [Several counselors told me how sorry they
felt for me while I was trying to speak over the din.]

Waddy summed up their attitude: Just keep your
cool and hang in there. This thing is having a pro-
found impact. I was surrounded by five big, tough-
looking inmates after the night service. They said,
"You're new with this group, aren't you?" "How did
you know that?" I gulped. They said, "You look
frightened." "That's only because I am," I told them.
They laughed, and man, was I really sweating. [He
mopped his bald head to the laughs of his fellow
counselors.]

The next day I awakened early. I was nervous and wondered
if we had been fooling ourselves the night before in our
testimony session. Sam Bender and I had breakfast together in
the dining room of the motel. We were in the middle of our
meal when Paul Anderson arrived. Paul wanted to know how
it had gone the first day. When we told him, he roared, "Oh,
you're havin' trouble, are ya? Praise the Lord! I always like it
when it's rough. We'll see if we can't handle this. When's my
clinic?"

"Well, you'll be on about one o'clock this afternoon." "I'll
handle 'em," Paul replied. He always likes a challenge!

I was secretly glad that I didn't have to go out until about
noon. The other counselors and special guests were going out
for the morning athletic clinics. The basketball clinic was being
led by McCoy McLemore. He'd played with the Milwaukee

Bucks until his recent retirement. Now he is coaching at Rice University. I had met him for the first time the night before in the motel, and was very impressed. A really good-looking guy, he is clean-cut with a direct, pure look in his eyes. He also is committed to the Lord. "A little naïve," I thought to myself as I looked at him. "I hope these guys don't chew him up and spit him out." Still, he had one thing in his favor that I didn't: black skin.

When I arrived at the prison, I was told that McCoy's basketball clinic had turned out well. There were a lot of basketball enthusiasts in the prison. Attendance was excellent and there had been little heckling. A similarly positive report came on the baseball clinic. Bobby Richardson, the former All-Star second baseman of the New York Yankees, was well received. Bobby is one of the most articulate of the Christian athletes. Very serious and businesslike he has a certain presence that discourages opposition. He made lots of friends that day.

Paul Anderson was on first in the afternoon. Jim Houston, former Ohio Stater and a teammate of mine on the Browns, and I were on at two o'clock. I was glad Anderson was going first. He grabbed the mike and bellowed, "I'm the strongest man in the world! At least, that's what they call me. I picked up 6,250 pounds and in the *Guiness Book of World Records,* they say that's the most any man ever lifted. I want to talk to you about weight lifting and physical strength." He grabbed a handkerchief out of his suitcase, and a two-by-six. "I used to ask someone out of the audience to lend me a handkerchief to prove that I didn't have anything in it," he said, "but the other day, I asked a guy for a handkerchief and he had a cold. From then on, I started bringing my own. But as you can see, it doesn't have anything in it." He flipped it around in the air to show that it was just a plain handkerchief. He folded it several times and put it inside his hand. Placing a twenty-penny nail in his hand and jerking it up above his head, he drove the nail into the two-by-six. It came out on the other side with at least an inch showing. He held the nailed board up in the air so that everybody could see.

"Hey, man, what do you weigh?" an inmate yelled. Paul replied, "three hundred seventy-five pounds."

"You sure look fat," a con needled.

"All of the heavyweights have a little fat, but most of my bulk is muscle," he insisted. The inmates agreed by applauding. Those who tried to heckle, Paul ignored.

He normally took only about twenty-five minutes for his demonstration, and saved more for the night service, but this time he took a full forty-five minutes and held the audience spellbound.

Jim Houston and I quickly followed Anderson with our football clinic. There were some distractions while we were doing our clinic, but not enough to bother. Paul had settled them down.

In the night service, Paul Anderson picked up where he had left off that afternoon. The inmates were again very respectful and attentive while he spoke. I followed him without interruption again, so that they wouldn't have a chance to change their mood, but as soon as I got up, they began to make noise. It was obviously organized. They'd watch the demonstrations, but wouldn't listen to the gospel. I forged ahead, praying for the words which the Lord would have me speak. As I talked, an amazing thing happened—the audience began to listen, really listen. Most wanted to hear and they subdued the hecklers. The more enthusiastically I spoke, the more the inmates were with me. By the time I was through with my speaking that night, it slowly dawned on me that the hecklers were helping us! Their plans to destroy the whole program had backlashed. Even some of the inmates that couldn't have cared less about what we were saying were listening because they disliked the interference. Isn't there a saying about honor among thieves? Well, by and large, these guys, I discovered, had a sense of fair play.

Afterward, the inmates surrounded Paul Anderson and me. They were asking for our autographs and expressing appreciation for what we had done. As I glanced up, I saw that our counselors were busy talking to the inmates.

Jerry Lundgrin came running up to me after that Saturday

evening service and said, "Bill, you've gotta come down to the infirmary with me." Jerry is a dentist from Salina, Kansas. He had come to know Christ on the last verse of the final invitation of the final night of our city-wide crusade in Salina, only a year before. Now he was coming with us on prison crusades.

Jerry has a perpetual smile on his thirty-five-year-old face that makes him look even younger than he is. But now his smile was even broader. At the same time, tears were welling up in his eyes and spilling down his cheeks:

> "I promised him you'd come see him," he said. "Settle down, Jerry, and tell me what's up." "You remember the guy who got stabbed last night in his cell as we were coming into the institution?" "Yes," I responded. I'd heard about an inmate being stabbed four times.
>
> "They have him in the infirmary all sewed up," Jerry reported. "I went down to talk to him, and he has committed his life to Christ. I want you to meet him, Bill."
>
> A couple of minutes later in the infirmary, I was looking into the young man's face. He looked like a college freshman. The multiple stab wounds made it difficult for him to move, but he had a big smile when he recounted his conversion.
>
> "When I got back here to the infirmary after being sewn up, I felt terrible," the man said. "For the first time in my life, I prayed. I said, 'Oh, God, I would like to meet someone from the crusade group in the prison.' It wasn't five minutes until Dr. Lundgrin came into my room. He said to me, 'I'm from the Bill Glass crusade group. Do you feel like talking a while?' I said, 'Sure, I was expecting you.' He led me to faith in Jesus Christ. I am so pleased because God has forgiven me."
>
> I asked the guy (I'll call him Mike) if I could pray with him. He said he'd like that. First I thanked

God for his saving grace, then I asked him to give Mike the strength he'd need since being reborn. Then Mike prayed: "Lord, thank you for sending these people to show me how I could find your forgiveness. Thank you for answering my prayers. Thank you for giving me new life." When Jerry and I left the room, he wasn't the only one with tears in his eyes.

What would cause Jerry Lundgrin to leave a beautiful family and give up a restful weekend for three days in prison? When I asked him, here's what he told me:

I had grown up in a Christian family. My grandfather was a minister, my mother has been in church work for many years. She teaches Bible classes. I thought I had Christ in my life. I'd been associated with him ever since I can remember, but I hadn't taken that first step of salvation. I hadn't asked him to come into my heart. When the Bill Glass crusade came to Salina (October 15–22, 1972), my wife bugged me to go and I went the first night. She asked me to go back the second night, but a pro football game was on TV, and I copped out of that one. After that, for the next six nights, she kept after me to go back with her. To please my wife, I ended up going. She kept saying, "Jerry, I want to go down and make a commitment, but I'm not going unless you go." I refused. Finally, it came down to the last verse of the last song of the last night, and she said, "You know I need to go down," and I said, "You go on, Honey. I just don't feel moved." They were singing and Bill reminded us of the Bible's warning, "If you are a stumbling block for anybody, it's better that you had a millstone put around your neck and be cast into the ocean." I realized right then that I was a stumbling block to my wife. Bill pointed right in my direction—I thought it was right at me. He said, "If

you don't know Christ, you're not fit to be a father."
I nudged my wife and said, "I'm ready. Let's go." By
this time, everybody was leaving for the counseling
room, and we went around the back way. I got ahold
of a young counselor and told him everything he
wanted to know. I faked him out. Just like in basketball, you can throw all those fakes, but unless you
score, it doesn't count. Well, I hadn't scored. The
counselor took me to where Sam Bender was standing. I guess a lot of people had been praying for me.
Sam asked me about my decision. I said I got this
warm feeling while I was sitting there. "That's
beautiful," he said, "When did you accept Christ?"
I said, "I joined the church when I was twelve." Sam
said, "When did you accept him into your heart?" I
said, "Maybe you and I better sit down right now and
get this job taken care of." That did it.

Soon we were back in the motel at the nightly sharing session. Jerry Lundgrin told about Mike's experience, but Charlie
Spross told a story that was even more difficult to believe.

I'll never forget the first time I met Charlie Spross. It was on
a cold, wintry day in 1971. I was to preach in the very proper,
very formal First Congregational Church in Toledo, Ohio.
Their building is beautifully ornate, so much so that it seemed
more Catholic than Protestant to a guy who grew up in simple
surroundings. On the inside, there are high arches on both
sides, tremendously high ceilings—Gothic architecture. The
pastor was dressed in an Anglican robe. However, he agreed to
my giving an invitation. It was the first invitation that had been
given in that church in a hundred years. The congregation was
attentive. As I very carefully and apologetically gave the invitation, I was astounded to see that the aisles were filled . . .
soon, the entire front of the church was jammed. I suggested
that everyone go to the church parlor. There, we had a number
of committed Christian counselors who shared their faith with
those making decisions. One of the persons responding to the

invitation was Charlie Spross. For many years, Charlie had been a top amateur golfer, winning the Toledo District Championship several times. He attended church on Sunday mornings, and that was about it. He really didn't know what it was to have a vital relationship to Jesus Christ. But all that was soon to change. He began to grow by leaps and bounds. He attended all the prison crusades with us. He became very active in the follow-up at Marion and other institutions where we had worked.

Now he was on his feet speaking to this group of counselors and special guests. "I also heard about the young man who got stabbed. But I started thinking about the one who had done the stabbing. He was in the hole, maximum security."

"I'd like to get into maximum security," Charlie had said to the captain. "Why?" the captain asked. "I'd like to talk to a man in there." "No way," answered the captain, "They're a bunch of animals. They'll tear you apart, attack you, spit on you. They'll throw their food on you. They're not interested in what you have to say." Charlie persisted, "I still want to go in." Several other counselors were with him and added that they wanted to go in, too. One of them standing with him was a counselor by the name of Orville Fricke. We had gotten to know him in our Marion crusade. Orville had been an inmate at Marion when we were there. Since paroled, he was now serving as a counselor with us. Finally, the captain agreed. But another guard warned, "Go on in, but you'd better keep your hands out of the cells. Don't shake hands with them. They may jerk your arm right off your body and beat you to death with the bloody stub."

Spross explained:

> The place was dark . . . the kind of place that was too cold in the winter and too hot in the summer. The ceilings were low. Naked pipes outlined the ceiling. Everything was concrete or stone. The first cell I came to I looked in, and in the darkness, as my

eyes got acclimated, I could see a stark-naked black man. The cell was about six-by-ten feet. There was no bed or anything . . . just four concrete walls, ceiling, floor, back and sides. The front wall was bars. Remembering the warning, I hesitated to stick my hand through the bars. But I knew I must at least try to shake his hand. I knew if I didn't trust him enough to stick my hand through the bars, he would never be interested in what I had to say. I introduced myself, "I'm Charlie Spross, and I'd like to meet you." Poking my arm as far as possible into the gloomy cell, slowly the man came forward, grabbing my hand in the soul handshake. When I risked sticking my hand through the bars, he responded. I really didn't have any fear at the time. Maybe a little later, but not at the time. He really said nothing. He didn't mention his name, but grabbed my hand. His hand was damp and warm. I began to talk. "God loves you and has a better plan for your life." It wasn't long until he began to seem interested. He didn't make a commitment to Christ, but the Lord was really working on him, and I knew it. During the conversation I discovered that he was the one who had stabbed Mike.

On Sunday morning we all met in the gym. There were theater-type seats, and they were elevated above the gym floor. The speakers and other program participants stood at floor level. The inmates came in lesser numbers on Sunday morning. Many of them were sleeping in. Yet there were still about five or six hundred. The counselors were scattered throughout the audience as usual. It was sprinkling rain outside. When Bob Cole gave his testimony the inmates were attentive to what he had to say, and there was virtually no heckling. Luckily, most of the hecklers were among those sleeping in that Sunday morning. Then it was Pete Redmon's turn. He did a very effective solo, "Ship Ahoy," and then ex-con Orville Fricke stood up to give a testimony. Only a few months after his parole from Marion, he came to Mansfield Ohio State Reformatory by special arrangement to act as a counselor for us.

I'd like to tell you what Christ means to me. I know what you are going through. For the past seven and a half years, I spent most of my time where you are. I was in Lewisburg, Pennsylvania Federal Penitentiary when I decided I really couldn't hack it—on my own. I was in a dormitory they called the "jungle." And it was! There were fifty to sixty fellows in there. I'd never been confined in my life before. I had a home for boys—my wife and I—for delinquent boys from ages fourteen to twenty. I never dreamed I would be put in such a corner. When we ran out of funds I was determined that the home wouldn't fall. So I got involved in some things that were questionable and I got caught. You can see, I was a miserable failure. I was scared to death in that Lewisburg dormitory. I couldn't sleep. No one here can tell me they aren't scared to death the first time they go to prison. I really decided I couldn't handle it. I said, "Lord, there's nothing I can do on my own. Forgive me for what I've done. Use me from now on for your honor and glory." I slept like a baby after that. I didn't fear anyone in that penitentiary. When you make a decision for Christ in prison, you'll be laughed at, you'll be jeered. Brother, hang on. This makes you strong. Christ came into this world to die for our sins. He paid the debt for us. I've thanked God many times for the opportunity of being in prison. I'm not proud that I went to prison, by no means. But I am glad that I got to go there and tell other men what Christ has done for me. My heart bleeds for every one of you men. Every one. I don't care who you are or what you've done. The love of Jesus Christ in my heart makes me love you. I love you, brothers, and you'd better believe it. I'll do what I can to help any one of you. Don't think being a Christian is an easy life. When you get out of this institution, don't forget the men who are here. They will be in the same condition that you are now. These men need help and if we as ex-convicts would have done this years ago, we would have conditions in prisons much better.

In Archbold [a small town in northwest Ohio], I've got the best job I ever had in my life. I'm foreman there in a factory. The community has accepted me well. I've been speaking to quite a few churches to explain prison conditions. Society doesn't realize what goes on in prisons. If the judges and lawyers knew prison conditions they wouldn't send as many men here as they do. How can we change things around? A lot of so-called Christian people on the outside should go to court and try to help. I'd say 75 percent of the fellows in these institutions should not be here. A little help from a Christian man could get this man straightened out—and he'd never have to spend time behind bars.

Rehabilitation in prison? There's not one in one hundred rehabilitated in prison. All you learn is other crimes that you never dreamed of before. People try to drag you in on schemes that they have. You've got to be a man to stand up for what you believe. A Christian gets laughed at, scoffed at, made fun of. But this is good. It makes you strong. When people see you're not just doing this to shoot an angle for the parole board, that's when they respect you. What did the Bill Glass crusade in Marion do for me? It gave me backbone, to start with. I looked forward to the follow-up program with Charlie Spross, Gus Yeager, and the men from the Toledo area.

I've got to be pretty careful. The state opened the doors for me to come in at Mansfield, which was unheard of a few years ago. I mean, a man coming back into a prison while he's on parole. Right now, I'm working with a man who has been on drugs for eighteen years. I got him out. His wife left him, his family left him. He didn't have anything left to live for. We got to talking. He was probably the most filthy-minded, foulest-tongued man I knew at Marion. I kept showing—not only in words—but showing what Christ meant to me. This, in turn, changed his life around. He has committed his life to Christ. Christ will do the same for you.

We had had good attendance at the rock concert on Sunday afternoon and I had followed that with my final message. One of the things that really seemed to get through to the inmates that afternoon was when I said:

In the eleventh chapter of Hebrews, I read the roll call of the saints. These are the saints of God down through the centuries. These are the greatest men of God that have ever lived. Yet, if you catalogue all the crimes that these men have committed for which they could be committed to prison, you'll discover there are murderers, robbers, thieves, people who committed adultery, fornication, bigamy . . . every crime you can think of was first committed by the saints of God. What does this mean? Does it mean God uses convicts to accomplish his purpose? Precisely, that's what it says. He doesn't want you to remain a convict. He forgives you for your sins and uses you to accomplish great things. God's in the business of taking a guy who has really hit bottom and using him. In fact, a guy has to hit bottom of self-trust before he can be used. You have to recognize your need before you can be helped. A man who doesn't recognize he's sick doesn't go to a doctor. Be-

come aware you're sick spiritually, then you can be
helped.

You guys have a great advantage. You realize your
need. The dying thief on the cross said, "Remember
me when you come into your kingdom." He wasn't
any great theologian. He recognized he had a need.
He was just a dirty, dying thief. He fulfilled every
requirement—he acknowledged the ability of the
Lord to help him and he turned in faith to the Lord.
The Lord responds to those who ask.

But now it was time to leave. As we were saying our final
good-bys, inmates were lining up to get autographs in their new
leather-bound *Living Bibles*. Tyndale House in Chicago had
given these to our organization. Sam Bender had been in
Chicago and made an appointment at Tyndale House only a
couple of weeks before. They had agreed to send us a thousand
of these Bibles to give to the men at Mansfield. The inmates
couldn't have been more pleased. Many of them were expressing their appreciation. "This institution will never be
the same," one black said. "I can't believe it. Blacks and whites
actually shaking hands, and calling each other 'brother,'"
another one agreed. "Are you going to do crusades like this in
other institutions?" another con asked.

"Sure, we are going to continue to do these all over America,"
I answered. I thought to myself, "If he'd asked me that a couple
of days before I don't know what my answer would have been.
Right in the middle of that first message with all that heckling,
I was almost ready to throw in the towel."

Finally, it was time to leave. I signed autographs as the
guards hustled the inmates to move along. As we were entering
the cellblock building, the inmates were being herded into their
cells. There was a line of inmates just getting ready to go up
the steps in front of us. Pete Redmon was walking to my right,
talking to one of his inmate friends. He had his arm around
the inmate. This is a privilege that is only earned after the
inmate totally trusts a counselor.

Suddenly, a voice called out from the line of inmates. It was Lefty Dog. Breaking ranks, he ran to Pete and shook his hand with enthusiasm. Then he whispered in his ear, "I just wanted you to know . . . my name is Frank. And thanks, you've really helped me." Then, "Will you write me?" Lefty Dog called as he was moving back into the line-up.

"Yes!" Pete shouted back.

Yes, Pete observed later. The man was no longer a left out dog. He was a man, and had a name to prove his worth. He hadn't become a Christian, but he was shown love and respect. He was appreciative and open. Rather than our biggest opponent, he was now a friend.

Waupun State Penitentiary

Chapter Seven

Once a month our executive committee meets. We usually have the meetings in a dining room of an office building in downtown Dallas. Garry and Jack Kinder, Jim Ray Smith, Bill Brashears, and I made up the executive committee at that time. It was June of 1973, following the Mansfield prison crusade.

Bill Brashears was anxious to tell the committee about his experience at Mansfield. He started by saying:

This was the first time I was able to be a prison counselor. It was just before lunch, and they were getting ready to run the inmates back in for a head-count. I was sitting in an area between two cellblocks, which is kind of a no-man's land. This area is only large enough for a couple of benches. I was sitting on one of the benches when a young inmate came up and sat down with me. We began to talk about Christ. He had a lot of problems. I wanted so badly to talk to this young man, but as I started to share Christ with him the guards hustled him back into the cellblock. That afternoon I couldn't find him, but before we left the institution I managed to get his cell number so that I could find him sometime later on in the weekend.

The program proceeded on Saturday with athletic clinics all afternoon and the crusade service that night. I had a number of inmates that I was supposed to see. There would be no possible way I could see them all in one night. So I chose the ones that I thought were most important to see. Although I hadn't talked to this young guy long, God impressed me that he was the one I needed to see most. Perhaps it was because of the sense of insecurity he seemed to have. I stopped at his cell first. I sat down and started to talk with him. His cellmate, one of the older men in the institution, was with him and they both had Bibles. The cell was designed for one inmate, but there were two in it. In a cell this small, only one could be out of the bunk at once. So the young inmate was sitting on the floor and his cellmate was sitting on the bed. As I shared the gospel with them, they were obviously under conviction. The one I'd originally come to see told me how he'd been in and out of institutions since he was seven years old. He was now just twenty-two. He had no one on the outside but his grandmother, who had raised him. He was in prison this time because he had been working at a McDonald's restaurant when he became angered at his boss. He kidnapped one of the girls who worked there and robbed the cash register. He told how some of his imprisonment had been in mental as well as criminal institutions. It was obvious that he had a wealth of problems.

I talked at length with both of the men about the Lord. It was getting late by this time and the guards had begun to hustle the counselors out of the cell-blocks. I had gotten to know the guard in charge of this range earlier in the day. His wife was from Abilene, Texas, and since I was from Texas, we had something in common. He told the other guard, "Let this man stay as long as he wants." I was allowed to stay there about thirty or forty-five minutes after everyone else had left. I shared the Four Spiritual Laws with the inmates. Both acknowledged that they would like to accept Christ. With difficulty, they both managed to get out of the bunk and onto the floor where they knelt. I was on my knees outside the cell. Both men had tremendous conversion experiences. Tears of rejoicing flowed among us.

I have received letters from both men since then and they are studying and trying to grow in the Lord. It was quite an experience to see both of them on that tiny floor space, weeping and asking Christ to change their lives.

The committee members sat enthralled listening to every word that Brashears had to say. I reported to the committee the progress of the entire prison ministry to this point:

Well, we've finished three crusades now, and each one has taught us a new lesson. Marion and Tehachapi were much alike. At first, they were relatively cool but warmed up quickly and were very responsive. Mansfield followed the same pattern but a great deal more drastically. There was yelling and screaming throughout every service, but it tended to lessen as the weekend went on. Even during the demonstrations, all except Paul Anderson's, there was loud heckling. However, we discovered that the heckling ultimately gravitated in our favor. The inmates began to get mad at the very few who were heckling and listened more attentively than they otherwise would have. It seemed they were listening in spite of the hecklers. Even at Mansfield, there were over five hundred decisions out of the eighteen hundred inmates. Well over a thousand inmates have responded in the three crusades. I am definitely against counting scalps or putting a great deal of emphasis on numbers. However, it is exciting to realize that that many inmates made commitments and at least prayed to receive Christ or made some other kind of definite commitment to the Lord. The counselors filled out cards on each inmate they counseled. The follow-up in the institutions is going beautifully. The amazing thing is that even our financial picture is growing better, though we have spent a great deal on these three crusades. The prison gang is at least starting to catch on now and people are getting involved in the total ministry. Our city-wide crusades have been going great and they have contributed to the outreach in the prison ministry.

I guess I would have to say in summary that though this crusade at Mansfield appeared to be more volatile and dangerous than any of them because of the great number of young inmates, it turned out to be the best of the three we've done thus far.

Before I knew it, September 14, 1973, had rolled around and I was on my way to Waupun Prison in Wisconsin. Unknown to me, the warden, Ray Gray, had many reservations about the crusade coming to his institution. It was a tinderbox of emotion, and had been considered such since 1965. At that time there was a bad riot. That had been the last time the whole prison population was assembled in the yard at the same time. Now we were going to do it again and the whole community was nervous.

The prison chaplain called Jim Carley, who was the prime mover behind our coming to Waupun. Jim Carley was an intense and successful businessman. We first met in Cleveland at a Christian couples' club meeting where I'd been the speaker. A good-looking dude in his mid-forties, he breaks all the molds. Spiritually an evangelical, he is a political liberal with strong commitment to social action programs. Carley had been the big man in our Madison, Wisconsin, city-wide crusade. In fact, he had, at times, carried that crusade on his back—financially and organizationally. On the board of Inland Steel, he also ran a construction business in Madison. One of his social action programs in Madison was a halfway house for teen-age boys. It had had its problems. The changes that came in the lives of the boys were few and in many cases short-lived. Jim saw many kids end up in prison and decided something needed to be done about rehabilitating them. He was really excited about the prison ministry because it combined Christian witness with social action. As a counselor at Tehachapi, he had seen the Lord change many lives, and he was determined it would happen at Waupun.

Prison chaplain Bill Counselman was calling Carley to report on the upcoming crusade at Waupun. He said, "I have been told that riots are being planned and Satan-worshipers are up in arms here in the prison. Everybody appears to be uptight . . . inmates, guards, administration, and above all, we chaplains. We've been getting calls from everyone about the fact that the grapevine has it that there'll be a riot. I've stuck my neck out and told the warden how great it is going to be and how nothing is going to happen. Since I walked into this prison four years ago, I've been praying for something like this to happen. But I honestly fear all hell will break loose. A few phone calls and threats like I've been getting aren't going to stop us. I want you to know that things do look pretty shaky here, Mr. Carley, but we are going to have a great crusade in spite of it all."

I'm sure glad that no one told me about all of this. Otherwise, I would have been uptight and probably less effective. Sometimes it's better not to know.

Jim Carley picked me up at the airport when I arrived in Madison, Wisconsin. It was an hour's drive to Waupun, Wisconsin. Jim was very optimistic. When I asked him about the money for the prison crusade, he said, "I told you I'd raise the money for this crusade, but I'm afraid I've failed. I'll pay for it myself. I've just had too much going lately."

I was flabbergasted! It would cost a bundle. We had to pay honorariums and travel expenses for all the athletes. We would buy two meals for the forty counselors.

"Come on, Jim, you shouldn't have to pick up the total tab," I protested.

"Yes, I will," he replied.

Ray Gray, the warden of Waupun, was a paradox for me from the start. I didn't know how to rate him, pro, con, noncommitted, not interested, afraid to tip his hand.

He greeted me in the prison reception room shortly after I arrived. Gray wore glasses and was of medium size, about 5–11, I'd judge, and about 200 pounds. He appeared to be a little nervous, but assured us that he was pleased for us to be there in the institution and would be accompanying us all weekend. That meant he was totally interested or totally untrustful. I didn't know which. "You know, Bill," he said, "this is the first time we'll have all of the inmates together in the yard at one time since 1965. We had a big riot then."

"If you're trying to make me nervous," I said half-joking, "you've succeeded." There was more.

The warden was saying to me quietly, "These men are 40 percent murderers. Most of the rest have also been involved in the most serious felonies—armed robbery, assault, rape—you name it. You know this is the maximum-security prison for the state of Wisconsin, so we get the tough ones."

The Friday afternoon program came off without a hitch. The inmates, about 600 of them, enjoyed our exhibitions and behaved themselves admirably. The evening service was also well attended and well received. At the reporting session back at the motel, the counselors had many stories to tell of inmates who accepted the Lord. Others told of inmates who expressed interest and wanted to hear more. The counselors had arranged or planned further meetings with these men. But as always, part of the fascination came when I heard the stories of the counselors. Their reasons for coming and how they'd come to serve the Lord were every bit as exciting as the inmates.

For example, Harvey Strassburger's story inspired us all. He was from Madison, Wisconsin, and had served before as a counselor with us at Marion. My first contact with him came at our Madison city-wide crusade. There he decided he would find out more about our organization by coming to the prison crusade in Marion.

He explained in quite excited tones:

> As we were walking among the inmates down to the prison yard tonight, I spotted a familiar face. I couldn't place him at first.
>
> "Hi," I opened nervously to the inmate who stood only a few feet away. He nodded, but walked hurriedly on. As the inmate walked toward the bleachers I searched my memory. Suddenly, it came to me. I had been on the jury that had found him guilty three years before. Not only that, but I'd been the foreman of the jury for the trial. The man I'll call Jimmy Pearce was charged with the murder of a woman strangled to death. Pearce was black; the woman white. So there were some racial overtones to the trial. The prosecution charged him with first degree murder.
>
> Pearce was from Mississippi, I remembered. There were eighteen children in his family and he seemed mentally slow. Still, he showed nothing of a violent

nature. The woman whom he allegedly murdered had lived in the same apartment unit as he did, according to the prosecution. One night he approached her, made sexual advances, but the woman rejected him. According to the prosecution lawyer, this angered him and he strangled her to death.

The jury had a tape recording of his confession to the murder which clinched the case. When the jury reached its decision, it fell on my shoulders to announce, "We, the jury, find the defendant guilty as charged." He was sentenced to life in prison, which meant a minimum of eleven years. That's the minimum sentence in the state of Wisconsin for murder.

I was sitting with the inmates in the bleachers while you spoke, Bill, when Jimmy Pearce, of all people, came and sat down beside me. After you gave the usual invitation to accept Christ, I began to talk with the young man. I knew I hadn't confused him because I recognized his face and when he introduced himself, I remembered his name. He gave no indication of recognizing me, however. I decided not to tell him who I was, but just to witness to him. I followed along with what you said in your invitation, Bill, and asked him if he would like to know more about how to become a Christian. He said yes, and I led him to faith in Christ.

I thought at first that I wouldn't tell him. I feared that he might react badly, but I somehow felt that I must tell him. I would be coming back for follow-up work. So, I told him who I was! He hadn't recognized me, but it didn't make any difference. He wasn't bitter at all. "You just did your job," he said quietly.

Such irony! God had used a man who had a part in taking Pearce's physical freedom away to lead him to a new spiritual freedom.

It was about as strange as the story about another counselor named Bob Rowan of Wilkes-Barre, Pennsylvania.

Bob's interest in prison work came as a result of an experience which nearly cost him his life. A retired pilot and businessman, Bob had led a rip-roaring life full of worldly pleasures before he found the Lord a few years ago. He also had built up quite a fortune, which he used to finance his high life-style. It was this accumulated money that led to a bizarre event that rivals a Hitchcock movie thriller.

Bob had invested a great deal of money in mutual funds with a local broker-friend whom he trusted implicitly. However, the man suffered severe financial reverses and through a ruse got Bob to sign over his portfolio to him. Then, to cover his tracks, the broker hired a gunman to do away with Bob. Under the guise of showing him a lake property in a desolate area outside of Wilkes-Barre one night, the broker got Bob in position for the professional killer.

But an incredible thing happened. After a bloody fight and a bullet-firing chase, Bob was subdued in a woods. The gunman stood over him, his loaded pistol poised to squeeze the trigger. However, the shot that would have ended Bob Rowan's life never came.

Lying helpless on the ground, Bob remembered something his mother had told him long ago. Worried that her son might die in a plane accident, she counseled that if ever he were the pilot of a crashing plane that he should ask God to forgive him for his sins. "If you do," she said, "he will forgive you and you'll spend eternity in heaven."

Bob was not the slightest bit interested in his mother's faith then, but when he thought he faced imminent death, he recalled her instructions and hurriedly he petitioned God. For some unexplainable reason, the hired killer lowered his gun and walked away.

Badly injured, Bob made his way to help. He recovered to testify against the pair at a trial months later. At the trial, the hired gunman testified that he had been overcome with a strange and sudden nausea as he stood over Bob in the woods that night, and it was that repulsion with the act he was about to commit that made him change his mind. Bob had an explanation. It was at that instant he was saying the prayer his mother had given him.

In the end, Bob came to accept Christ and when he did he forgave his assailants. As proof of his forgiveness, he visited the convicted gunman regularly in prison and eventually helped lead him to Christ.

Paul Anderson was in rare form at Waupun. Dressed in a new bright orange suit, he looked like an overripe Valencia orange. His sport shirt gaped open, revealing a hulking, hairy chest and a cross necklace made of two rough nails. Looking out on a sea of faces Saturday, Paul drew his 375-pound frame together and bellowed:

"I was driving around this place trying to find the entrance today, but I couldn't. So I yelled up to one of the guards in the tower, 'Hey, officer! How do you get in this place?' 'You're the first guy that's ever asked that question,' he shouted back." The inmates laughed and applauded. Then he told about a kid who stole a car and hadn't gone two blocks until it broke down. "What did he do? He broke into a parts house and stole the parts to fix it. Now that's resourceful, the kid was thinkin', a little mixed up, but bright. I'd rather work with a kid like that than a guy who sits on his tail," Paul said. The prisoners were intrigued by Paul's acceptance of the boy. "He can be helped," Paul went on. "He's now one of the fellows in my boy's home in Vidalia, Georgia."

When he was through with his talk and exhibition, the inmates mobbed him, waiting to shake his hand. Several inmates turned to me to ask questions about Paul.

"Did he really pick up 6,250 pounds?" one inmate wanted to know. "Yes, that's what it says in the *Guiness Book of World Records*," I replied. "Have you seen one of the pictures of him on the posters around the institution? It's the one of him picking up the back of an automobile while they change the tires."

The inmates nodded that they had seen it. Then I told them

an unbelievable story that I had recently heard from one of Paul's friends. One day Paul and his family were visiting in a town close to his youth home. When he came out of an ice cream parlor with three ice cream cones in one hand, three teen-age boys sitting in the front seat of a late model Cadillac jeered. "Look at the fat man," one heckled. Continuing to deliver the ice cream cones to his children Paul seemed to ignore the boys. But he suddenly stopped and returned to the Cadillac. Taking the front bumper, he lifted the front wheels off the ground and placed the front end of the Cadillac over a nearby guardrail. The tires were about two feet off the ground!

Smiling, Paul made a low bow and rejoined his family. When he drove away the boys in the Cadillac were still in shock, their mouths open and their eyes as big as double dippers!

After we finally left the prison Saturday night, we drove to Chaplain Bill Counselman's home, an old frame two-story house, about three blocks down the street from the prison. Unlike other prisons we'd visited, this one was located in the middle of town. Bob Cole was so full of excitement he had to share:

> This afternoon, Chaplain Bill called several of us together in a little huddle behind the platform. He was most concerned about one special guy. "Bob, if you can reach one young man in here by the name of Harry Smart (not his real name)," he told us, "many of the other fellows will follow his lead." Harry Smart was a big, tall black, about 6–3, strong as an ox and mean as a junk yard dog. Harry had been sent up from Chicago on a list of crimes as long as Kareem Abdul Jabbar's arms. And he wasn't reformed. To let other inmates know he was ready for a fight, he wore an ace bandage on his hand for protection for his tools. To add to his image, he wore colored glasses. No question about it, he was the leader, the kingpin of the whole prison. The other inmates followed after him. So Bill Counselman said, "Bob, let's pray about

this." I agreed. We put our arms on each other's shoulders and prayed. As quickly as we said, "Amen," we looked up and there was a hulking black, practically in the circle with us. Bill was a little shocked and stammered, saying, "Uh, uh, Bob, shake hands with Harry Smart." I said, "Thank you, Lord. Hello, Harry. I have something I'd like to share with you." He said, "Well, first you have to do something for me." I answered, "Okay, what is it?"

"Do you see that guard over there?" asked Harry. I said, "Yes, I see him."

"He's put me on report because I didn't get in line. I want you to go over there and take my name off that list. I refused to line up a little while ago after one of the services."

I agreed to try, but I didn't have any faith that the guard would listen. But at least Harry might appreciate my trying, I reasoned, so I went over and talked to the guard. I said to the guard, "My name is Bob Cole and I've come from Lexington, Kentucky. It's mostly our fault that some of the men have been late lining up. Would you take Harry Smart's name off your list there and put my name on it. I'll be glad to stand his punishment for him."

"Oh, I'll take his name off," he said, "just tell him to straighten up."

That taken care of, I said, "Come on over here and sit down, Harry. Let's talk a little while." Harry asked, "Bob, why did you do that?" I said, "Well, Harry, that's sorta like what Jesus did for me. He took my sins and bore them all in his body. That's what the Scripture says, and I believe it. I know he did it. He put his name in my place. I should have spent a couple of lifetimes in prison." I told him I'd probably done more things wrong than all the inmates put together because I'd lived longer and was mean. But then I said, "All that's changed, and I'd like to introduce you to the One who changed me." I began to share the Four Spiritual Laws with him. I could see that he was disturbed. I could see that the Lord was dealing with him, but he read aloud right along with me. We got to the point where I asked him to pray and invite Christ into his heart. Just before I got a chance to ask him, "Where is Jesus right now in relationship to you?" he just blurted out, "I can feel him right now in my heart!"

"Thank the Lord," I said. "Would you like to pray again, Harry, and thank the Lord for saving you?" He nodded. Then he prayed and thanked the Lord for coming into his life. He went and got many of his buddies and like Bill said, they were willing to listen because Harry vouched for me. He really was the kingpin and it may have been the turning point in the crusade.

One of the men Harry brought to me was a contract killer for the Mafia. He was white and had worked in and out of Chicago and Milwaukee. He had been convicted for killing one of his runners who picked up money for him at a post office box. He knew he had to kill the runner to keep from being found out. So he killed the guy and got caught. He was serving time in prison for it now. I spoke to him a little while, and of course, God's Spirit was there. This man had been under conviction before I even talked to him. He had only one reservation about accepting Christ: his sordid past. "How in the world could I be a Christian? I've killed fourteen men!" he told me.

God immediately gave me insight and I said, "Man, God will forgive you just like he did David. David was a man after God's own heart. He was a multiple murderer." I had never thought about it before, but God reminded me that David, when he put Uriah, the captain of the host, to the forefront of the battle, he had gotten the whole host wiped out. This made David a multiple murderer. Lots of the things David had done were hideous. I told him that Moses was a murderer and Paul was a multiple murderer. "Well, then," he said, "I'll accept him if he'll accept me." And that's exactly what happened.

Warden Ray Gray and I were talking together toward the end of the crusade, and he said, "I was following all the happenings very closely. I could hardly believe what I was seeing. A crowning blow came, though, when one inmate rushed up to me and said, 'Warden, I want to thank you.' The inmate had never said anything positive in the five years he's been here. He was placed in the institution on a murder charge. And for all five years, every contact I've had with him has been negative. He's always cussing me or some of the staff about something. This man just has a sorry attitude, but now for the first time, he said, 'Hey Warden, thanks!'

"I couldn't believe my ears so I jogged to catch him, and asked, 'Thanks for what?'

"The inmate replied, 'Oh, for allowing this team of people in here to help us this weekend. They're for real.'

"I had to find out what you guys were saying to those inmates," Gray continued, "so I went to your counselor, Dave Templeton, and asked him, 'What are you saying to these cons in here?' Dave is an FBI agent whom I trusted. By this time the inmates had given Dave a title, The Christian Federal Fuzz. Dave said that everything was contained in the Four Spiritual Laws which he read to me. I was interested. But I really got double-teamed. Bob Cole closed the deal a little while ago. It's the greatest thing that's ever happened around here, Bill," he said. "I can't thank you enough." He had tears in his eyes.

He was afraid that he'd have a riot on his hands before we came. It turned out to change the entire atmosphere of his prison, and a life-changing experience for himself.

Templeton had his own story. He came up to me and said: "Bill, I don't know what in the world got into me crying like that."

"Like what?" I asked, and he proceeded to tell this story:

I was afraid. Maybe it was like Peter's experience when he tried to meet Jesus on the water. I had been recognized by a prisoner as an FBI agent on Saturday morning. I assumed from then on that I was a "marked" man. However, on Sunday morning the re- action of the crowd after my introduction to give my testimony was such that I was really taken aback and had some moments of fear. I think this fear was from the reaction and not really knowing what to expect from this crowd.

As he talked, tears began to course down his face, and the looks of hate in the audience changed to acceptance. The in- mates grew to love Dave. The guy that recognized him on the first day was a fellow he'd busted a few years before. Dave proceeded:

Joe Gonzales (name changed), also known as "Pedro," was serving concurrent time for local and federal charges. The federal charges were violation of the Monn Act, which means interstate transportation of prostitutes. All charges stemmed from a prostitution ring headed by Pedro, wherein girls were brought from Minneapolis, Minnesota, to Madison, Wiscon- sin, to solicit. I was the FBI agent responsible for put- ting the case together on the federal level and primarily responsible for sending Pedro up to do time.

He recognized me but wasn't hostile. We talked about lots of things and finally I spent about two hours with him going over the Four Spiritual Laws.

Dave didn't get Pedro to commit his life then. It isn't that easy sometimes. But he planted the seeds and a few weeks after Waupun, I got this letter:

My last contact with Pedro was a week ago, and he still has not accepted Christ. But he sent me a letter in which he stated the following:

"You made a lasting impression on all of us. You're the only fuzz in the penal history to move freely among the convicts without guards. It took a lot of guts for you to come inside this place and mingle unguarded among cop-hating convicts. The biggest dude in the joint is a cop killer. Situations reversed, I wouldn't have done it. Yes, chicken! Upon recognition of who you were, the first thought across my mind was, either this guy is a fool, or he really believes and is practicing what he preaches. If residents here hadn't really thought you were for real—a real Christian—there would have been one awful riot, with you in the middle. You wouldn't have made it out alive."

It takes courage to go into a situation like Dave did, but the results are astounding. They always are when we trust God and stick out our necks in faith.

Counselors preparing to enter Maximum Security— "the hole" at Kentucky State Penitentiary

Chapter Eight

There are so many amazing stories to tell—stories of changed lives as a result of our prison ministry.

There was Milo Choate's experience. He lives right down the street from me in Duncanville, a suburb of Dallas. He's about thirty-six years old, ruggedly good-looking with a black patch over one eye and a mustache. It was at the conclusion of a successful crusade, and the assistant warden of the prison was expressing appreciation for our work. Milo offered, "You know, I'd really like to talk to you. It could be that I could share some things with you that might be helpful." The man nodded his approval. Milo and the assistant warden descended two more flights of steps down to the ground level. I continued to stand there at the top of the steps, looking down as Milo had found light under a street lamp to talk with him about Christ. Not only was this man the assistant warden and the prison psychologist, but he seemed to be an extremely competent person. He had a church background, but did not have a vital relationship with Jesus Christ.

I was talking to Waddy and said, "Isn't that something, Waddy? We've got the greatest counselors in the world. Milo Choate has the guts to tackle a psychologist with the simple gospel plan." As we continued to watch, Waddy was saying to me, "Yes, look. He's gonna put the Four Spiritual Laws on him now." Sure enough, Milo had whipped out his Four Spiritual Laws booklet and was instructing the psychologist in the most basic Christian principles. Behind us were six stories of concrete, stone, and steel bars. One of the most awful institutions in the country. In front of us, a beautiful river shimmered in the moonlight. And far down on the street level, Milo and the psychologist were framed in the street light. I said to Waddy, "This has to be the height of satisfaction . . . to be a part of a ministry like this. Some of us planting, some watering, and others reaping the harvest." Several of the other prison officials were coming out of the building now, and we talked for some time. Waddy and I finally went down the final two flights of steps and into the street. Milo was motioning for us to come over across the street under the light with him. Milo said, "Bill I know you'll be pleased to know that our friend has committed his life to Christ."

Tom Joseph, a personal friend and veteran of many prison crusades, was sitting on the first row of the bleachers during a football clinic. Joseph is only medium-sized, but a well-built guy in his mid-forties. He was wearing cowboy boots and a Texas hat. He's a West Texas rancher. There were a couple of inmates sitting on either side of him. He had shared the Four Spiritual Laws with them and they had come to know

Christ. Then, two other inmates approached Tom and his two new Christian friends. They indicated that they'd like spiritual help. Tom said, "Well, these men here can show you." He handed each of them a booklet. "Now, just go back through the Four Spiritual Laws like I showed you," he said to the two new converts, "and show your friends how to receive Christ." So he sat back, crossed his legs, relaxed, and watched the new Christians introduce the two men to the Lord. Joseph said, "I felt ten feet tall seeing my converts winning others. Just think of it. I had spiritual grandchildren in a matter of a few minutes!"

A thin, Latin-American con with raven black hair came up to me. He was about thirty years old, a good-looking dude with a mustache. He said, "I must see you alone." He waited for the whole area to clear. "Bill, I haven't even told my psychologist this. I haven't told the chaplain. My wife doesn't know. I certainly didn't tell my lawyer. Can I have your word that you won't tell anyone?" "No one," I reassured him. His thin face wrinkled at the forehead and twitched around the eyes. He was talking out the side of his mouth. "I killed a man. They didn't have any way of proving it. Every bit of the evidence was circumstantial. I know you won't tell anybody. They could only get me in here for a couple of years. I'm going to get out in six weeks. Man will let me off—God will never let me off. I'll burn in hell for eternity." I don't know the man's name. Nor will I ever tell where or when I talked to him. He confessed to me as if I were a priest.

I tried to convince him that the Lord would forgive him. About the time I was getting started, we were interrupted by some other inmates. He slipped away in the crowd. I never saw him again. I don't know whether the guy ever did trust the Lord or not. He was terribly tormented. We have to remember that the people we were talking to have committed all types of crimes. We have to remind ourselves that all of us are capable of doing the same. You have to be unshockable. You can't have a self-righteous attitude toward them. Except by the grace of God, every one of us is as capable of the same horrible crimes.

I can honestly look at them as God's creation, not needing to be judged by me.

May 24–26, 1974, took us to Kentucky State Penitentiary at Eddyville. Bob Cole was the prime mover behind our going to Kentucky State. He had been very active in our city-wide in Lexington, and wanted us to go to at least a couple of prisons in Kentucky. The week before we had been to LaGrange, a medium-security prison. But now Bob had arranged for us to go to a maximum-security institution. Bob Kurtz, from our full-time staff, worked with him doing the advance work. This time I did get a forewarning of trouble.

"There have been several murders recently and one escape," Kurtz said. "It was a rather bizarre escape. This was the sixth prison the guy had been in, and he'd escaped from every one. The last breakout happened only yesterday. They had put him on the inside cell of the sixth floor. He loosened the bars in his cell. Throwing a grappling hook made out of bed frame steel up to the roof, only one floor above, he climbed to the roof on a rope made of bedsheets. Once he was on the roof, he climbed across to the opposite side and shimmied down the rope six floors. Still being at least ten feet from the ground, he dropped the rest of the distance. He is still at large," Bob said.

After clearing security, I was confronted right off by the most frightened, timid inmate I've ever seen. "Look, first off I want you to know I'm an agnostic. I just don't know about this Jesus bit. I'd talk about it I guess, but I'd rather not. What I really want from you is for you to talk to Bill Houchin. He is the head man of this joint and has the power of life and death over all the inmates. If you could reach him it would change the atmosphere of the whole place, but it won't be easy. He has killed four men with a knife."

"Sure, I'd be glad to talk to him," I said swallowing hard. I hope he doesn't make me number five, I said to myself.

"Where is he?" I questioned.

"He's in maximum security. I don't even know if they'll let you in to see him," the inmate replied.

I put the thought aside and went on with other business, but not fewer than ten cons asked me to visit Bill before the first day was finished. On our way out Friday night I said to the captain, who was escorting us, "I sure would like to meet Bill Houchin."

The captain said, "I think it can be arranged. When do you want to see him?"

"Right now," I replied. He was hesitant but said okay. Several counselors standing nearby asked to go along. We walked down a long sidewalk and into a corner. The buildings were arranged in a U-shape. The entrance to maximum was a small steel cage. Concrete was under our feet, but bars surrounded us on all four sides and top.

As we walked in, the door was locked behind us. We were counted, identified, and signed in. We were going to the maximum security of a maximum-security prison. Finally they opened the inner door and we walked into a reception room. There was still more. We went down another flight of stairs and into a control room. Another door was opened to us and we walked into what was called the "hole." This was where they kept the tough ones. They would endanger the lives of other inmates, or in some cases their own lives would be threatened. The place was poorly lighted. A few 40–watt bulbs hung from the ceiling of this basement cellblock. There were no windows, only solid concrete stared back at you from the ceiling, floor, and walls. Along the long, narrow room ran a row of six-by-eight-foot cells. Each cell had a commode without a seat, a bunk, one 40–watt lightbulb, and a sink. I wondered where an inmate took a shower. Finally, the guard pointed out Billy's cell. I walked over and introduced myself. He was genuinely glad to see us and expressed his appreciation in a polite southern backwoods drawl. His English was slangy, but he could communicate well and his mind was keen. It was obvious that he was a leader. "Why they got you down here, Bill?" I asked.

"I killed two in a riot here," he related, "so they shipped me off to Missouri. Up there I killed a couple more."

"Why did you want to do that?" I questioned.

"Well, they hassled me and we got in a fight. I really didn't mean to do it, but I guess I kinda go beserk when they hassle me." His nostrils broadened and his red hair seemed redder as he told how they kicked him around. He was stripped from his waist up and his curly chest hair matched the hair on his head.

He talked freely about all of his problems. However, he was most interested in sports. We spent the first ten minutes of our discussion talking about football. "I love the Cleveland Browns," he told me. "I remember seeing you play for the Browns. All the Browns' games were televised in our area. Football's my favorite sport."

I knew he was impressed with size and strength, so I said, "Paul Anderson is coming in here tomorrow to put on a weight lifting clinic and demonstration for the guys. I'd like for you to meet him."

"Would you send him down here to talk to me?" Billy asked excitedly.

"Sure I will," I said.

"I don't know whether they'll let you do that," he said.

"We'll sure try," I assured him.

We continued to talk for at least an hour. I tried to break off the discussion several times, but with pleading eyes he would continue. I just couldn't get away from him. Finally, the captain motioned for me to come on. I assured Bill that I would be back the next day with Paul Anderson.

When we returned to the main prison, there were about forty or fifty inmates waiting to get a report. "How's he doing? What did he say?" they all wanted to know.

"Well, he's OK. We had a good discussion. I'm going back to see him tomorrow."

The next day Paul Anderson and I went to see Billy as I had promised. As usual, Paul had won the inmates over with his weight lifting demonstration. But now I wanted him to meet the head man, Billy Houchin.

Billy was thrilled to meet Paul. "They tell me you drive a twenty-penny nail through a two-by-six," Billy exuded.

"That's right," Paul replied.

"Doesn't that hurt your hand?" questioned Billy.

"No, I wrap the head of the nail up in a little handkerchief and it keeps it from hurting my hand." Paul talked to Billy for a little while and then moved on to meet other inmates in the hole.

I sat on a little box right outside Bill's cell and we talked for at least an hour. Finally he said, "You know, I really would like to come to know your Christ."

"Well, Billy," I said, "I'd like for you to." His big rough face was sincere and I knew it. He was for real.

"I'm gonna do one of three things," he said with measured voice. "I'm gonna kill myself, kill somebody else, or commit my life to Christ. But I just can't continue like I am. I'm going mad down here. I've been locked up down here for nine months."

"Don't they ever let you out?" I questioned.

"Naw, never," he replied.

As we talked about committing his life to Jesus Christ, he began to cry. Tears began to roll down his cheeks and then he began to shake around the shoulders and neck as he sobbed. Finally, he said to me, "Let me think about it tonight, you come back tomorrow and we'll talk again."

"I'll be back, Billy," I promised.

Again, when I got back upstairs, I was surrounded by forty or fifty inmates asking, "What'd he say? What'd he say?" I said, "Well, he said he was going to do one of three things."

"What three things?" one inmate impatiently probed.

"He said he was going to either kill himself or somebody else, or accept the Lord," I revealed.

"Well, if he said it," one inmate said, "you can believe it."

"Tell us about him crying," another man said.

"How did you know that?" I asked. It had happened only five minutes earlier, and it was behind three locked doors in a windowless dungeon. "The vine," he answered.

Sunday morning at Kentucky State Penitentiary dawned gray
and rainy. We had to move the worship service inside, which
cut our crowd, but the inmates were surprisingly enthusiastic,
considering the weather. The chapel was full and many inmates
were just hanging around, hoping to hear part of it without
appearing too interested. We were told that many of the inmates who came to chapel that day had never been there before.
Others just refused to go into the chapel. It was stepping over a
line they vowed never to cross. Listening to testimony on the
recreation field was one thing, but going to chapel was another.

As usual, we had different counselors give their testimonies.
We always asked Bob Cole, who is a sales manager for a car
dealership in Lexington. The inmates were entranced by Bob's
words, which boomed forth from his 230-pound body like a
mighty wind.

He told his life story from his gut and he meant business.

> For thirty-six years the devil and I were buddies.
> You see, I was a gambler and a hustler. You can't
> cheat an honest man—it's impossible. But there is
> larceny built into every human being, and I nurtured
> it. Man, did I ever! I've sat in your seat. I've worn
> your shoes, and I know how you think . . . and
> how you feel. My heart goes out to you. I want to
> share the Lord with you. He loves you. He has some-
> thing wonderful in store for you. I know he can help
> you, because he saved a varment like me.
>
> It seemed like I was always waiting for ships that
> never came in. Now there is a Ship of Heaven for
> me. There is a Captain on that Ship, the Lord Jesus
> Christ, and you can meet him now, right in this
> place. I used to separate people from their money.
> I'd give a sucker two chances—slim and none. I can
> speak your language—I've heard you talking out
> there in the yard. I know the lingo! I know what
> they mean because I used them all, but while I was
> living that kind of life, there was something deep

within me—just like there is something deep in every man—that wouldn't be satisfied.

But something happened one day that stopped me in my tracks. I lost a billfold with $3,900 in it. A knock came at our door. It was a little old lady. "I came to return your billfold," she explained. I looked at her in amazement.

"My Jesus wouldn't let me keep the money that doesn't belong to me," she said. I couldn't believe it! I stole that money, she found it and it should have been finders-keepers. I asked her how she got to our house. She said, "On a bus." I offered to take her home in my car. She lived in a tiny apartment. I thought to myself, this little old gal has nothing and you have everything. For the first time in my life, I saw someone who had something I wanted that I couldn't take. As I was driving back home, I vowed to turn over a new leaf. That honest old lady made me take inventory of my bankrupt life.

I decided to work, of all things. I'd never had a regular job. Somehow God had said to me, "I'm still going to make a winner out of you. All you have to do is put up your sinful carcass and trust me. Will you do it?" I said, "Yes, Lord, I will." I got down on my knees right in the automobile showroom and entered into a verbal contract with God. And let me tell you something: Jesus is beautiful! He's real! He's alive! He's everything you've longed for and he's yours for the asking, gentlemen, right now.

Twenty-two of the inmates came to Christ that day.

When it was nearing time to go, I returned to the hole to see Billy Houchin for the last time.

Into the cage, back through the reception room and through the third door into the cellblock. Back on the little box outside Bill's cell I sat. He was ready from the first. He wanted to trust

Christ. "Okay, I'm ready," he said. "Show me how." I opened up the little booklet, Four Spiritual Laws, and proceeded very slowly to show him how he could become a Christian.

"It's that easy?" he asked.

"Easy as fallin' off a log," I told him. "Easy, but hard to mean it and live it."

"I mean it," he answered. That day he committed his life to Christ! After praying, there were tears in his eyes again. This time, a big smile broke over his face. A radiance. He had become a new creature. He was transformed. He had actually experienced new life! Now I was the one with tears in my eyes.

This time when I returned to the others, they again asked me to describe what happened. "Billy has become a Christian," I told them. They mumbled their disbelief. Even the nervous agnostic who first told me of Billy was pleased, and told me so as he grabbed me in a bear hug.

They couldn't comprehend how a tough like Billy could be reconciled with Christ, but the Bible is full of impossible conversions—Saul's, Zacchaeus', Nicodemus'. And the longer I work in prisons, the less surprised I am to see God work his miracles. I'm thankful He specializes in lost causes.

Roger Staubach passing, Bill Glass playing center in
Football Clinic at Florida State Prison

Chapter Nine

One of the biggest things that's happened since our prison
ministry began took place in Tallahassee, Florida, in May of
1974. We were there in a city-wide crusade. The general chairman of the crusade was J. T. Williams. We had first met in
Harlingen, Texas, eighteen years before when he was an air-
man at the base there.

Mavis and I were married in a local church and J. T. taught
Sunday school to junior boys in that church. One of the other
teachers in the department was Mavis' father, Parker Knapp.

J. T. is a short little guy who wears glasses and is every bit as intelligent as he looks. Warm and enthusiastic, he did a beautiful job in the crusade as general chairman. President of a large real estate development company, he was able to exert a lot of influence and get the community really with us in the crusade. He even arranged to have Governor Reuben Askew come to the crusade and give his testimony.

The services were held in beautiful Florida State University Stadium. As many as twelve thousand people came to a single service. Governor Askew was there on a Tuesday night. I was introduced to him by J. T. in a room beneath the stadium. Right away, the governor and I developed a rapport.

"J. T. tells me that you guys are having some revolutionary things happen in your prison crusades," the governor said. "Tell me a little bit about them." After I had outlined our program he said, "I wish you would come and put on one of these crusades in every prison in Florida. I would back you all the way." "Are you serious?" I asked. "Yes, indeed," he answered. I told the governor that I wasn't sure where the money would come from, but we'd try to go to as many prisons in Florida as possible.

As that crusade progressed, however, I came to realize that the most important person I'd met in Florida wasn't the governor—it was J. T. Williams. He had his business so arranged that he was able to get free to do a lot of work in our ministry, and I asked him to serve on our board of directors. But it wasn't until several months later during our Santa Fe, New Mexico prison crusade, where J. T. had come to serve as a prison counselor, that everything began to fall into place and I realized what God had planned.

By September of 1974, Sam Bender had personal difficulties that forced him to withdraw from working with our organization full-time. Bob Kurtz, our radio and television specialist and prison crusade director, had accepted a good offer for a television sportscasting position in Denver, Colorado. So, we were without a prison crusade director.

I decided we would go to Santa Fe State Penitentiary with Bill Carlson as the prison crusade director. He had come to

Cleveland four years before I retired to discuss his coming to work with me as a city-wide crusade director. I had never done a city-wide crusade at that time. But several people were talking to me about it. As things developed, he worked the last three years I played pro football setting up crusades for me. I'd work in the off-season and he'd work year round. When I retired, Clyde Dupin came with us to expand our ministry. Others joined the staff as the need increased. Bill Carlson had his hands full as our city-wide crusade director, but we had no choice.

We were staying in a Santa Fe, New Mexico, motel while conducting the prison crusade. Just that morning at breakfast, I'd been telling Carlson that I was thinking about hiring another prison crusade director. He had responded, "Maybe we won't have to. J. T. Williams and Jerry Lundgrin have a better idea." They had been discussing it with me and I suggested some possibilities to them. Late that night there came a knock at my door. I opened to see Williams and Lundgrin. They looked like they had a secret too good to keep.

"Gotta talk to you, Bill," Jerry said with urgency in his voice. "J. T. and I have some ideas to share with you." Then J. T. began to carry the ball. He started by saying, "We both have some free time. Though we have demanding businesses, they are in good enough condition to allow us to spend at least some time in this work. Why couldn't we take over the prison ministry? You no longer have a prison crusade director on a full-time basis. Sam and Bob have left and you are going to need someone."

Jerry Lundgrin had committed his life to Christ during our Salina, Kansas, city-wide crusade. He had introduced his first person to Christ at Mansfield, when he became the spiritual father of the boy who was stabbed four times by his cellmate. These two experiences were enough to weld him to our ministry. He had continued to act as a prison counselor in every prison crusade we had done since. He had grown continuously more enthusiastic about our ministry.

J. T. continued, "Look, we have an invitation to twelve prisons in one state—Florida! We have invitations coming in from all over the country to do prison crusades. We have no prison crusade director. We could go out and hire one, but that costs money. If Jerry and I took over the prison ministry and ran it for you, then we could do two or three more prisons a year than we could otherwise. The Association could take the money it would normally use for paying a salary for a prison crusade director and use it to do more prison crusades." J. T. finally ran down, looked at me intently, and said, "Well, what do you think?" I looked at Jerry, a successful dentist in Salina, then J. T., a six-figure executive.

"Well, the price is right," I said. "I don't imagine I could hire two executives of your caliber for less than a couple hundred thousand. You offer your time free, sounds awfully good to me! I'll bring it up at the executive board meeting and see what they say." Seven men from our board of directors sit on our executive board in monthly meetings. They make the day-to-day decisions for the total board, which meets only once a year.

Two weeks later at the executive board meeting, I told them about the Williams–Lundgrin proposal. They agreed. They were all for it. "But what are you going to do about Bob Cole and Pete Redmon?" board chairman Garry Kinder asked. "You tell me they are pivotal to the prison work, and if we make J. T. Williams and Jerry Lundgrin prison crusade directors, they might think they're being cut out." I nodded and told Garry we needed all of them.

After some discussion, we decided to go with four prison crusade directors—all of them laymen, and working as their own time allowed. I called each one on the phone. All four responded beautifully. They thought it was a good plan. If one didn't have the time, another one would. They were spread all over the country. That would help in checking out prisons and also responsibilities for crusades. Pete Redmon lives in Peru, Indiana; Jerry Lundgrin in Salina, Kansas; J. T. in Tallahassee, Florida; and Bob Cole in Lexington, Kentucky. With these four sharing the duties our prison crusade program took on more formal organization. They devised "check-out lists" to make certain all details were attended to. Have we arranged for a sound system? Have arrangements been made for Paul Anderson's table (the table on which the inmates sit while he picks them up)? Have we arranged for Mike Crain's watermelons and concrete blocks? Have we got footballs? baseballs and bats? basketballs? All other materials for the clinics? Will the warden agree to stopping all work programs during the crusades? Will movies that might be shown during the clinics or services be rescheduled so that there aren't any interferences? Four pages of detailed questions were covered in the check list.

The new prison crusade directors were featured in the next issue of the *Goalpost,* the newsletter of the Association. And, man, did they get after their new ministry with enthusiasm!

Their first prison crusade was in DeSoto Correctional Institution in Arcadia, Florida, near Sarasota. They had big plans for another one to follow very quickly thereafter. Instead of having one, they were going to have three at one time! I wasn't sure we could swing it, but I was not about to express any doubts. "Forget the torpedoes, full speed ahead."

Following the Arcadia crusade I sat down with our four new prison crusade directors and we mapped out elaborate plans for the Big Three to be held April 18–20, 1975. Among the things we decided was a radical new departure to try and satisfy the tremendous number of invitations. We would do three prisons at once. This would triple the number of inmates we could reach, and help us financially in that it would maximize our special guests. The travel expenses and honorariums would be the same for them, whether they did three prisons or just one. So, it would be very little added expense to do three at one time. Three prisons were chosen, which were in close proximity to a small town named Raiford, Florida, near Jacksonville.

On my insistence, they finally agreed to change the name of our crusades from "Bill Glass Prison Crusade" to "Total Person Weekend with Bill Glass and Friends." This sounded a great deal less egotistical to me, and I thought it would have a much better appeal to the largely secular audience in prisons.

Jerry Lundgrin enthusiastically interrupted to say, "I think the best thing we've ever had is this spiritual enrichment time we had here." Bill Carlson was the leader. He conducted it much like we do in our city-wide crusades. The counselors had gathered at 9:00 A.M. The motel had furnished us a room in which to meet. Carlson had spoken for about an hour on spiritual commitment. The second hour he encouraged us to share problems that keep us from being the kind of committed Christians that we ought to be. The honesty of the sharing time was beautiful!

One counselor confessed to the group:

At Eddyville in the orientation session, Bill, you said, "You must love every inmate. You disqualify yourself from helpfulness to the men behind bars unless you have love." When you said that, I bowed my head and prayed, "God, help me not to talk to that con who recently walked into a house in my home-town. I can't possibly love him. I hate him. He killed four friends of mine, and when they asked him why, he said, *Just for fun.*" I consoled myself by saying that I wouldn't be very likely to talk to him anyway. Too many men in this prison. Only one chance in fourteen hundred that I'd have to talk to him.

When Bill was talking to Bill Houchin, I was two cells further down talking to an inmate. The cell was dimly lit. The man was bearded and drawn. I didn't know who he was, but we talked at length and finally he committed his life to Christ.

I asked his name so I could put it on his decision card. When he gave it to me, my heart sank. This was the inmate whom I prayed the Lord wouldn't let me see. Then I prayed silently, "Oh, God, help me to love this man in spite of what he did." I know you won't believe it because I couldn't believe it my-self, but my heart was flooded with love. I guess the Lord is a specialist in that because he did it so beautifully at the cross. I looked at the man as a father

would look at his own son, in real love. I honestly can
say I had no hate whatsoever left in my heart—only
love. It was like a huge needle was rammed into me
and all the hate was sucked out and replaced with
love.

Following the sharing session during the spiritual enrichment
time, we devoted a couple of hours to orientation. "We need
to do that same thing in the Big Three Crusade," Jerry persisted. Everyone agreed. Raiford, Florida, was less than an
hour's drive from Jacksonville. No sooner had our planning
meeting broken up and we left for home than we were all back
in Florida for the Big Three!

Jerry Lundgrin would lead the group doing Union Correctional Institution and Pete Redmon would captain the team
going into Receiving and Medical Center. J. T. Williams and
Bob Cole took the group going to Florida State Prison. Each
counselor group numbered just under fifty.

Again, we spent the first hour in spiritual enrichment time,
and another hour in orientation and spiritual enrichment in
three separate groups. I rotated between the groups, seeking to
give each group encouragement and support. This occupied the
entire morning and part of the afternoon, but by 2:30 P.M. we
were on our way to the institutions.

People magazine had sent a photographer and writer to cover
the weekend. *People* had picked two Florida guys to trail along
with me for three days. They were competent pros, so naturally
they were constantly asking probing questions and taking pictures. I knew this exposure would be great for our prison ministry so I enthusiastically tried to help them.

What a great team of counselors we had. There was Harold
Treece. He was about the size of a small split-end receiver but
had grown big in his heart. Harold is from a small town in
Kentucky called Elizabethtown. He's a member of a Methodist
church and had made a fresh commitment during the crusade
in Elizabethtown. He goes with us to all of our prison crusades
as a counselor. He wasn't always such a great counselor. He

confided in me, "The first person I talked to on my first prison crusade volunteered that he had killed his father. This shattered me. I wasn't prepared for it. But he found his salvation that afternoon." Harold and many of the other counselors had quickly matured from "being shattered." They'd developed a staunch faith. They had seen God work miracles through changed lives. They were confident of the Lord's ability to forgive the most terrible crimes.

There was Dick Osborne with his little peculiar golfing cap on. He was most skeptical in that first prison crusade in Marion, but now he was one of our biggest backers.

Of course, the four that stood out in the crowd were Williams, Lundgrin, Redmon, and Cole. They were doing a fantastic job as the prison crusade directors and were giving us about a quarter of their time.

George Joslin—he beats them all! An inmate walked up to George in Lewisburg Federal Penitentiary not too long ago, and said sarcastically, "If your God could get me out of this place and over that wall, I'd listen to what you have to say about him." George fired back, "Well, in the first place our God didn't get you in this place. But if he wanted to, he could get you out. I'm sure he wants more than anything else that you get right with him." The inmate replied, "I've got two sins I want to commit before I can become a Christian." "What two sins are those?" "I want to kill two men," he responded. "Why would you want to do that?" George asked. The inmate replied, "Well, they are the reason I'm here." "You like this place?" George questioned. The inmate quickly responded, "You know I don't like this place . . . I hate it!" "Then why do you want to come back here?" retorted George. "I don't want to come back," the inmate said. George replied, "If you kill two men, that's where you'll end up." "Yes, but they'll never catch me," the inmate responded. "That's what you said when you robbed that bank and got put here in the first place," George said.

If I ever had to go to war I would sure like to go with a bunch of guys like these. I felt like I had gone through some real battles with them already. We had shared in lots of victories.

Bunny Martin was there with his Yo-Yo and bag of magic. Since Mansfield he had been a regular for us and had continued to impress inmates all over the country. Our athletic guests were better than ever. We had added some excellent musical talent. It was a team effort and God was blessing it in a magnificent way.

To top it off, we had Roger Staubach, veteran of many years in the NFL and superstar in his own right, to do our football clinic. I had never been so proud of a team. I felt closer to these guys and loved them more than I did any world championship team I'd ever played on.

The most peculiar audience we ever faced was at the Florida State Prison. The morning of the football clinic, the audience was divided into three parts. On the other side of the outer fence was the minimum-security unit. It was about a hundred yards away from the outside fence of the prison. About 150 inmates from the minimum-security unit were sitting on the grass just outside the double chain link fence. They weren't allowed inside Florida State Prison, the maximum-security portion.

Staubach and I were now on the platform (a trailer truck bed), beginning the football clinic. There was a semicircle of chairs with about 250 or 300 inmates in them. Several others stood around in the back. The public address system was set up and we were demonstrating football plays for the inmates. What a peculiar audience. 150 just outside the fence, 300 right in front of us, and several hundred others still up in the cell-block buildings, unable ever to get out of their cells. But they could hear because the sound was blaring. Roger Staubach was talking to his audience about quarterbacking. The inmates were interested in what he had to say.

He answered questions thrown at him by the inmates. The microphone was draped loosely around his neck by a mike cord. The electrical cord dangled down by his new Dallas Cowboy shorts. Soon we were down off the platform and among the men, demonstrating passing techniques. I played center for him and snapped the ball. He would fade back and throw a pass to an inmate.

There were several pretty good receivers. They cheered wildly when one of their friends caught a pass, and booed when they dropped one. Most of them were in their late twenties and early thirties, and a few much older. Some acted like children . . . yelling and jeering if an inmate friend tripped and fell. But they were having fun.

Roger was most impressed by "Murf the Surf." He had been involved in the celebrated Whiskey Creek Murders. Before that, he robbed the New York Museum of a couple of million dollars worth of jewels. The Star of India Diamond was in that loot and it alone was worth a half million. He was a good-looking thirty-five-year-old man. He wore a regular inmate's uniform, all except for his alligator shoes. They were a holdover from his days on the streets. Murf tells his story like this:

My parents were good people who constantly promoted church to me. As a child I went to church . . . I went to this church, that church, and in moving as much as I did, I was constantly in different kinds of churches. I was a musician back then, playing the violin. I used to play in churches all the time. In fact, I've played here in prison on several occasions. So church is nothing new to me. I was aware of religion, of all those people reaching up for God, and of the whole atmosphere of Christian people. That is why later on in life I always knew that there was something there.

Anyway, as I grew older, I moved back East. I was going to the University of Pittsburgh. I had graduated from high school in McKeesport, Pennsylvania, and left that area and went to Miami Beach. I don't think I could have gone to a worse place because I got to Miami Beach really immature, spiritually. I looked around and people were down there just partying and having a fantastic time. So I figured if it's good enough for these people that come every couple of years to party, I was going to be here all the time! These people had money—they had success. They were possibly correct in what they were doing. They were chasing the all-popular American dollar, so I got caught up in that as a young person. I was influenced by all that I saw around me. Everyone had a big car and the women had mink coats. They were at the bars and at the race tracks and the parties. Miami Beach was one continual party!

So I got swept up in it and worked on the beaches. I was a tennis pro, a dance instructor, and a swimming teacher. I sold real estate and I traveled all around the country as a high-tower diver. I was an acrobatic driver with a troupe of entertainers. I worked with the Barnum & Bailey Circus and the Shriners' Circus for crippled children. I did the boat shows, the sportsmen's shows, and television shows all over the country.

I was constantly chasing, constantly having to go outside myself for my happiness. I would get up in the mornings and say, "Wow! Let's get a six-pack of beer. Let's go down and get some chicks. Let's go someplace and get this happiness. If I get that car I'm going to be happy." Then finally I was in business—surfing business—but I was chasing, still chasing. I ended up back in Miami Beach again. I was in a crowd of people whose activities were not legitimate.

I had a great deal of animosity toward people and society—toward everyone—because no matter where I went, I could not find that happiness, that peace. I had money, I had cars. I was married several times. I had all these things that other people had, but something was missing. There was a great void in my life.

I could look around and see that other people had that void in their lives, too.

I got into crime as an adventure, as an escape, as another avenue of pursuing pleasure. That pursuit led me to prison in New York, California, here in Florida and jails all over the country. I had to come this far. I had to come to the belly of hell to find peace, to find Jesus Christ!

[I questioned, "Why the name?"] That name was dropped on me years ago by the lifeguards on Miami Beach. During the hurricanes back in the fifties I was one of the few people around with a surfboard, and I would always be out in the ocean in places where the waves were extra good. The police would come and try to get everybody out of the water but the lifeguards would say, "Don't worry about him. That's Murf the Surf out there." It was sort of a joke —a nickname. I was a spear fisherman, a water skiing instructor, a scuba instructor. I was always associated with the water, so that name sort of stuck for years and years. When I went into business, that was the name of the surfboards we manufactured.

He and Roger had good rapport. They were about the same age, quick-minded, and intense young men. Murf was interested in Roger's overly-large second finger on his right hand. He had jammed it on a lineman's helmet while throwing a pass —not once, but a number of times. The knuckle was over twice the normal size. The three of us stood talking—Murf, Roger and I. Murf asked to look at Roger's ring more closely. Roger handed Murf his championship diamond ring. One of the inmates kidded, "Is it safe to hand a diamond ring to a diamond thief?" Everyone laughed, but Roger seemed a little uneasy, as now the ring was being passed through the group. Everyone wanted to see it. In a little while the ring was returned to Roger and replaced on his finger. Roger became so interested in talking to the inmates that after his hour was up, I had to almost force him out of the prison. He felt like I did. He wanted to give these inmates more and more.

Finally, he grabbed the mike and said, "If any of you would like to have an autographed picture of me for yourself or anyone you know, children or otherwise, I'd be glad to send it to you. Just give your name and address to Bill or one of his workers. I'll send them out right away." I feared that Roger didn't know what he was getting into. This could be a mammoth task. Inmates came up to me by the hundreds, all handing me addresses. Other counselors working with us got innumerable requests also. Every inmate wanted one for himself, his children, and friends. Roger said, "Don't worry about it. I've got a full-time secretary and she can handle it for me without any trouble at all."

I finally had to grab Roger by the arm and pull him out of the gate. As I was doing so, I was thinking about how he had told me on the way to the prison that there was no way he could stay very long. He had pressing appointments back in Dallas, there was a plane leaving at two, one at four, and one at six. He must get back. I said, "Well, it would be tough for you to get back on the two o'clock plane, but you can make the four o'clock one without any trouble." Now I was having to force him out of the prison to meet our schedule. We had another appearance at Union Correctional Institution at 10:30 A.M. It was 10:15 now and the inmates on the outside of the fence from the minimum-security unit were also wanting Roger's attention. They, too, were asking for autographed pictures. He stayed and talked with them for a while and our driver drove the car up beside the fence where we were talking to the inmates, we stepped in and rode away to Union Correctional Institution.

By the time we cleared security, it was 10:40 and we were late. The inmates were waiting for us. Five to six hundred of them were milling about in the recreational area. Mike Crain had just finished his judo and karate clinic. I grabbed the mike and introduced Roger. The inmates applauded and then we started all over again with our football clinic. After the clinic was over, I again had trouble getting Roger out of the prison in order for him to have time to make it to lunch and get to the Receiving and Medical Center by 1:30 P.M.

All three of these prisons had about 1500 men in them. To be late or to miss any one of them would have been tragic. It was shortly after 12:00 by the time I was able to pry Roger loose and out of the prison.

We found a Dairy Queen type restaurant in the small town of Raiford. We sat at a back table and Roger was dumbfounded. He couldn't believe the appreciation the inmates expressed to him for his generosity of time and friendliness. That was the least he could do. "I only wish I could do more," he explained. I had had a long and deep respect for Roger, but now it was greater because I could see his sincere compassion for the men in prisons. He wanted further briefing about the Receiving and Medical Center.

By now, Roger was totally unconcerned about his plane. He was saying, "I'll just catch the plane at 6:00. I want to spend more time in the Receiving and Medical Center. At 1:30, we were clearing security. We got to the recreation field, and found ourselves surrounded on three sides by a huge crowd of inmates. The bleachers were set up around us in a big horseshoe. The horseshoe was about fifty yards across. A trailer truck bed was in the open end of the horseshoe. There were at least 1300 inmates in the bleachers and sitting on the ground inside the open area of the horseshoe. We started the clinic on the trailer truck bed, but again quickly moved down into the area in the middle of the crowd for the demonstration. The men seemed excited about the clinic. It went well over an hour. Roger threw passes to the inmates and answered questions. I did my usual pass rush demonstration, then Roger said, "I want to tell you that the most important thing in the world isn't football." He then briefly but clearly told about his own relationship with Christ.

That night, the buses from the three institutions brought us all back to the motel for dinner and for a report session. The buses and cars for the special guests and myself arrived at different times over a period of about thirty minutes. Everyone was thrilled about what had happened. Our first two days in the Big Three Prison Crusade had problems, but seemed to be an overall success. There were 150 of us jammed into the banquet room and we were eating enthusiastically. Prison food is never good. These men had only prison food to eat that day, so they were really very hungry. Afterward, we opened it up to testimonies. Everybody would share what had happened to them during the day. We had a public address system in the front so I invited everybody to line up and share their interesting experiences from their first day.

The last man to speak was Jim Franklin [not his real name] —a tall, thin guy with sharp features who appeared to be in his mid-fifties:

> I have been a Christian since I was a teen-ager. I was so determined that my son would be a Christian. I devoted myself to him. I thought I was a good father, but evidently I wasn't a good enough husband. My wife left me. When she left, she took our son with her. He was only twelve years old at the time. In the divorce proceedings, she retained custody of our child. I got to see him periodically but never as often as I wanted to.
>
> It wasn't long after our divorce that our son began to get into trouble. I was heartsick and panicked at first. I had given this boy everything I had and now he was going the wrong direction. I loved him desperately. He was my only son. One thing led to another and he got in worse and worse trouble. I was always visiting him in some prison or jail or county facility all over this state, and several others. I've stood in the rain waiting to see him outside some jailhouse or in a prison waiting room for the last twenty years. From the time he was about thirteen or fourteen years old until he was thirty-two, I've visited him almost weekly. I wrote him several times every week. I called him when I could. He was always in jail

somewhere. I spent nearly every dime I had on lawyers trying to get him out of trouble. Everything I
tried seemed to be to no avail. He would promise me
faithfully never to get in trouble again, but he always did.

Four years ago, I was tired . . . desperately tired
of his being in trouble constantly. I made a rather
rash statement to him, but I know it was God's will.
I said, "If you ever get in trouble again, I'll never
visit you in jail. I'll write you, but I'll never look at
your face in jail again. That doesn't mean I'll stop
loving you, but I just can't bear to look at you behind
bars." It became more than just a rash statement. It
was a covenant with God! He assured me he
wouldn't get in trouble again.

Three days later he was involved in a holdup. His
partner shot a man. The dying man's wife pulled a
gun trying to defend her husband. My son shot her.
The man died; thank God, the woman lived. But my
son was still an accomplice to murder. He is now in
Florida State Penitentiary. I came up here this weekend but I still haven't seen him. In fact, I've driven
halfway here fifteen or twenty times. Then I would
remember my covenant with God and to Mike that
I would never look at his face again in prison. I'd
turn around and go back. I wanted more than anything else to see him. I would write him, but I
haven't seen him in four years. I pray daily that he
will come to know Christ and his life will be changed.
I'm still praying that he will come to know the Lord.
[At this point, Jim broke down and started crying.]
Would you pray for my boy? [That was all he could
say.]

I looked around the room and I saw many men with tears
welling up in their eyes. I said, "Gentlemen, let's stop and claim
the promise of Matthew 18:19: If any two of you shall agree

on earth as touching anything whatsoever, you shall ask and it shall be done for you of your Father which is in Heaven. This group is going to agree together on earth that Jim Franklin's son will come to know Christ. Let's all bow our heads, hold hands, and pray that God will save Jim Franklin's son tomorrow."

We prayed earnestly. Somehow, I felt sure that the prayer would be answered.

I spoke first at the Receiving and Medical Center on Sunday morning, then to Florida State Penitentiary to close out. Frank Kaczmark followed me with a testimony.

I first met Kaczmark in Madison, Wisconsin, where we were conducting a city-wide crusade. Every night, he would bring a different group of inmates from the city or county jails to attend the services. He was about 6–1 and thirty-five years old. He had a mustache and was ruggedly handsome. But best of all, he talked the inmates' language. He used all of their slang freely throughout his presentation of how Christ had come into his life. He was already a committed Christian, but had a terrible background.

He had been in prison twelve years of his thirty-three-year life, but he had committed his life to Christ two years before and that's when he began working in penal institutions. He told me that he had been in jail all over the northern states and even in Alaska.

He had been a junky, and he said that everywhere he went he would run into pushers and other junkies. Even in Alaska, he ran into Eskimos that were "shooting up" with heroin. But in "the hole" of an Alaskan prison, he'd begun reading his Bible. He finally realized that what he needed was a relationship with Christ. He had an experience with the Lord almost without human instrumentality. Now he was anxious to fight against Satan, drugs, crime, and work for the Lord. He accompanied us to our Waupun prison crusade. He did such a beautiful job in counseling inmates because of his prison background that we decided to take him with us to other prisons.

Bill Brashears who had been a second-string quarterback at

Texas A & M in the early sixties was now a stockbroker in
Dallas, Texas. He tells this story about Frank's Sunday morning
testimony at the Receiving and Medical Center:

> Kaczmark was giving his witness and I was sitting
> off to one side. In my line of vision to the platform
> there were two inmates. They were laughing and cut-
> ting up. They really acted like they could relate to
> what Frank was saying about drugs. Of course, Frank
> uses lots of drug and prison terminology that is com-
> pletely foreign to me, but they could understand him.
> As he talked, they stopped the horseplay and started
> listening. When Frank was finished he walked off
> the platform and was immediately surrounded by a
> lot of inmates. These two guys jumped down from
> the bleachers and ran to where he was. Frank was
> telling one guy about Christ, and the others were
> standing around. After some discussion, Frank asked
> this guy if he would bow his head and pray to receive
> Christ. When he did, nineteen men joined in the
> prayer and received Christ. Kaczmark said, "I ex-
> pected to hear one guy pray, but there was a whole
> chorus!"

But back at Florida State Prison, two men were most concerned about Jim Franklin's son. Jerry Brooks, a friend of mine
and brother-in-law of Bill Brashears, was also from Dallas. He
had come to know the Lord only a few months before his wife
came to work with us as financial secretary in our Dallas office.
His wife became so interested in our prison ministry that she
got her husband excited about the possibility of going with us
on one of the crusades. Jerry was double-teamed because his
brother-in-law, Bill, had served as a counselor for most of the
prison crusades since Mansfield. Bill Brashears was so excited
that Jerry just had to go along on the Florida expedition. Jerry
looks like an old high school guard. He's not that old; he's in

his mid-twenties. He's a little overweight, with pudgy cheeks, a ready smile, and a nervous laugh. But Jerry Brooks is a committed Christian.

John Mosher, from Lexington, Kentucky, a small bundle of laughing energy, with glasses that usually sit crooked on his face, was the other man.

Brooks relates:

The next morning was Sunday, our final day at Florida State. We got on the bus and I noticed Jim Franklin sitting in front of me. His large but thin face was distinguished by a prominent nose, but it was now wrinkled with concern. John and I had talked about it and had decided that before we left the prison that day, we'd talk to this man's son. At least we'd explain his options with Christ. I put my hand on his shoulder and said, "I promise you that John and I will witness to your son today!" He smiled in appreciation but was too emotional to speak.

We didn't know exactly how to go about finding Mike Franklin. There were so many men in that prison—some 1500. Jim Franklin said, "I want more than anything to see my son come to know Jesus Christ, but I don't want to see him myself. I want you two men to talk to him. If you can get my son to accept Jesus Christ, then I would like to see him. But if he doesn't, I don't want to see him."

So we talked to Austin Brown, the assistant chaplain, and explained the situation. He agreed to do his best to get Mike down.

Austin Brown had been in prison twelve years himself. He's now the assistant to the chaplain and he's free. He's a nice-looking black, short of stature, friendly, and excited about everything that was happening. Austin said, "We'll have him down here." John and I tried to pin him down to a definite time.

He said, "Around 11:00." So we waited. Jim stood in the background because he didn't want his son to see him. He would cry and pray. John and I had gone to the altar and prayed together and claimed this man's son. We asked the Lord to give us the words to say to him.

You could see Jim standing off in a corner, afraid they would bring his son down ahead of time and he would see him. This would spoil the covenant he'd made with the Lord. He made certain that he stayed out of sight so that anyone walking through wouldn't see him. His son could come down at any time. We waited until about 11:00, but still no sign of Mike. I asked them again and they told me not to worry, that he would be down. They explained that they were having trouble clearing it but he would be there. We had activities that we were attending . . . testimony worship service, Bill's last message, the rock musical group, and other things were all going on that morning. But between events, we would return to the chapel to check on Mike.

Finally, just after lunch, he came down accompanied by a guard. They said, "This is Mike Franklin." He was tall like his father, but heavier. He appeared to be much more muscular. He was dark-complexioned with a prominent nose. He was handsome and appeared to be in his mid-thirties. We introduced ourselves to him, and told him we'd like to talk for a while. He said, "What for?" John blurted out, "Because we want to talk to you about becoming a Christian."

"How did you get me out?" he persisted. "We just talked 'em into it." We walked into a small room about two times larger than a cell. It had a lot of books neatly catalogued on the shelves that lined the walls. There was a small desk with three chairs. It was the chapel library. A big glass window faced the entrance hall to the chapel. We could see out as people passed and went in and out of the chaplain's office across the hall.

Mike responded, "Well, my dad is a Christian. He's been trying to get me right my whole life. But not me . . . there's no way for me. You guys are wasting your time. You're barking up the wrong tree even talking to me. Didn't they tell you I shot a woman? She almost died. My partner in the holdup shot a man and he *did* die. I'm in for attempted murder and accomplice to murder. Man, they threw away the key on me. There's no way. You're just wasting your time with me."

By this time, Mike's eyes were flashing. He was communicating his despair as best he could. Mosher said, "Man, I was an alcoholic. They threw me in jail from Lexington, Kentucky, to Shreveport, Louisiana. I was the sorriest man alive, but Christ forgave me." Mike still couldn't accept the fact that the Lord could just forgive him. He wanted to get a certain level of *goodness* before he could ask the Lord to forgive him. We explained what Jesus was all about, and that he couldn't reach a plateau of goodness.

I continued, "One thing I'm sure of . . . if you ask, the Lord will forgive you." Then he, John, and I got down on our knees.

In the meantime, Mike's father sat outside in the chapel. He still hadn't seen his son, but he was praying. Man, was he praying. He had his head on his crossed arms on the pew in front of him, hunched over leaning forward, half-kneeling, half-sitting, and he was crying, "Oh, God," he sobbed, "if you'd only save my boy. You know how much I love him."

Mike was on his knees now, sobbing his repentant

prayer. "Oh, God, forgive me, forgive me, forgive me . . ." That was all he could say. Finally, I got him to ask Christ to come into his heart.

John Mosher was so thrilled that he leaped to his feet, flung open the door, and ran out into the chapel. Down the aisle he ran to a front pew where he found Jim Franklin almost down between the pews now, still sobbing and praying. John is a rather dramatic guy. He had tears rolling down his face, and as usual, his glasses were crooked on his head. He grabbed Jim Franklin by the shoulders, pulled him up into the pew back into a sitting position. Looking into his face, he said, "Your son is now in the arms of Jesus!" Jim Franklin was speechless! He sprang to his feet, ran down the aisle, and back to the room where his son was still praying with Jerry. He stopped, as if on the edge of the Holy of Holies, and he crept quietly up to the door, and placed his arms against the outside trim of the door. He leaned his body into the doorway. His skinny frame filled the entire doorway.

I looked up through my tears and I was still in a kneeling position with my arm around Mike. I saw Jim Franklin framed in the doorway. Mike looked up and saw his father. This thirty-six-year-old man seeing his dad for the first time in four years, leaped up and they embraced. Mike cried, "Daddy! Daddy! I found Jesus!" Jim's overly long arms draped around his son. With his hands, he patted his back, rocking back and forth as he must have done when the boy was a baby. "Son, I've never, ever stopped loving you!" Jim sobbed into his son's ear.

Both counselors stood watching and weeping just as much as father and son. Neither John nor Jerry tried to cover up their tears. They had never cried so freely and unashamedly since they were children.

Mavis Glass counseling with inmate at Lowell Prison
for Women in Florida

Chapter Ten

I had been jogging in the park near Waikiki Beach in No-
vember of 1975. Now I was walking at a brisk pace back toward my hotel. As I panted for breath, a young, dark-skinned
Hawaiian smiled sympathetically at me. A beautiful blue surfboard was balanced comfortably on his muscular shoulder. He
wore only a loudly colored bathing suit.

"Surf up?" I asked.

"Beautiful, man," he answered.

"Is it dangerous?"

"Can be," he replied.

"But not for the good ones, huh?"

"We had a pro from South America in the islands recently," he told me. "He was riding the crest of a twenty-five-foot wave and came down sharply on a coral reef. Killed him instantly."

"What's the most fun for a surfer?" I queried.

"Shooting the tube," he replied.

"How's that done?" I asked.

"Well, you ride the top of the wave," he began, making the arc of the wave with his free hand, "until it begins to lap over you and you go right down the tube of the wave. It's like being in a beautiful crystal cathedral. The sun sparkles down through the water and it's all around you. The noise of the thundering surf is deafening, and the speed is breath-taking."

"What if you lose your balance and fall?" I asked.

"It's like being in a huge washing machine—tumbling helplessly to possible death or injury," he answered.

I often wonder why people get so turned on about prison ministry. As he talked, I realized it's the same kind of thrill as "shooting the tube." No amount of time, money, or personal danger is too much. Those who play it safe by sitting on the beach may get a casual thrill, but they miss the thundering excitement of entering the arena and getting involved.

There are some who would follow the advice of Gamaliel (Acts 5:34). He advised that rather than beating the apostles or killing them for preaching the gospel, the Sanhedrin should only sit and watch. "If they be of God, we don't want to fight against God," he said. "If they be of Satan, they won't last anyway."

Therefore, he prudently suggested that the Sanhedrin simply sit and watch. This seems to be wise advice. But, this is always the advice of the Sanhedrin. The scribes and Pharisees are those who sit in the warm sun on the beach. They watch from the grandstands. They never really get involved.

The New Testament Christian approach, however, is to get in the action with everything you have and are. To "shoot the tube" for the Lord.

That is what is so exciting about our prison ministry. People are no longer sitting on the beach in the sun, picking up shells. They are out in the deep water, in the thundering waves, risking all for the glory of God. There are no Gamaliels among our prison crusade counselors.

At a recent board meeting, several reports revealed the thrills my co-workers have had "shooting the tube." One was Art Svedberg, former Cleveland heart specialist, early board member, and a close friend, who recently moved to Fort Myers, Florida, to become a doctor in a retirement village. He decided the very thing that some of these people, who literally sit on the beach and watch the world go by, needed was to "shoot the tube." So he brought several of them along with him to act as counselors in our DeSoto Prison Crusade.

I must admit that I tried my best to stay away from Pete [Redmon] while we were there in the DeSoto Prison in Arcadia, Florida. I knew he'd be looking for follow-up help. I had my hands full at the retirement village. I knew I lived closer to the prison than anyone else. Sure enough, though, he caught me and asked, "Art, would you lead a follow-up group here for a few months?"

Pete got me in that weak moment and I consented. Pete, I've never thanked you for it, but I'm glad you asked me. It was over a year ago. We have two groups for follow-up; one goes back each week. It's about 150 miles round trip every Friday night. We leave about 4:15 and get there about 6:15. Friday is Chaplain Steele's day off, but he is so impressed that he's there waiting for us every Friday.

Several months ago, one of the fellows asked a counselor, Len Paret, "Len, what does your wife look like?" Len tried to describe her to the inmate, and said, "Well, I have a picture here in my wallet." Little Rickie, the inmate, looked at her picture and said, "Could I have this picture? I want to put it in my room." Len told him that it was the only picture he had of her and he really didn't want to give it up. Rick said, "I don't blame you for that. But if you could get a picture of her, I'd like to have it."

Later on the way home as Len was telling me about this, I said, "Why don't we all bring our wives up here with us some night?" We weren't sure at first whether it was a smart thing to do, but we talked to our wives and they wanted to come. So we asked them to do some baking before the next trip. Twenty-three of us got together and went to the prison. There were wives and husbands and one little widow lady from Shell Point (the retirement village). She's about seventy-four years old, and she just couldn't wait to get in that prison. We had cakes, brownies, cookies, and all sorts of goodies. They had baked pounds and pounds of things, and we thought the guys could keep what was left over and eat on it for a few days. We got there and there were forty-five of them waiting for us. We instructed our team to mingle with the inmates and sit with them. We told them it was their responsibility to make friends with the inmates.

There were six inmates who couldn't come till later on in the evening. We decided we'd eat first and then have a testimony session. We told them to please not take too much so that some could be saved for the other guys coming later. We thought there was too much for them to eat at one time anyway. We gave them a napkin to go through the line with. They came out with goodies stacked like hotcakes! They ate some of everything. They never get homebaked things, because it can't be received into the prison. In about twenty minutes, everything was gone. We asked, "Do any of you fellows want to tell what Christ means to you? Do you have any comments about the crusade you had here?" Chaplain Steele piped up and said, "All they want to know is when is Bill coming back with that gang again?"

Then a black inmate got up to speak. He paced up and down telling how much he thanked the Lord for Chaplain Steele. He said, "I want you to know, you visitors here, that our chaplain takes four or five of us every week to his home. He's got a wife and a teen-age daughter at home. If I were in his place, I wouldn't take any of us guys to my home. I just wouldn't do it." He continued to thank Chaplain Steele for trusting them, and he gave a testimony about what the Lord had done for him. Then some others witnessed. In nothing flat our time was gone. All of the fellows lined up at the door and bowed and shook hands with the ladies. They told us how much they would look forward to seeing us the next week. They really meant it. I was thinking that I had never seen twenty-three people so happy. I've seen them since then, and they just can't get over it. They are like all of us who've gone in for the first time—they didn't see what they expected to see. I know prisons are filled with guys who've done bad things, but I still say that they are filled with good guys.

There are now sixty Christians in the prison, compared to ten when we first went there. We don't talk about doctrinal subjects when we are there for the study sessions. But several new Christian inmates were talking recently and one said, "I want to be baptized." They read the Scriptures and talked about it together. There was a swimming pool in the prison, but there was no water in it. So, they decided they would have a regular baptismal service in the drainage ditch. These guys got together and read the appropriate Scriptures and baptized one another, eight of them, in the drainage ditch. This was all done on their own—none of us were there.

The retirement village people have discovered that it's a lot more exciting out in the big waves shooting the tube, not without risk or cost, but much more satisfying!

Problems are so overwhelming in prisons. There is so much need you tend to throw up your hands and do nothing. So we decided to at least try to help in some areas of great need. Whatever we did would be at least some help. We can't solve all the problems, but there are some things we can do. One problem is contact with the outside world. Inmates have almost none.

I have often written inmates and they would say in their replies to me, "Your letter is the first one I've gotten in five years," and some say "ten years." One even said "fifteen years." I began to think about the fact that some of these inmates may never get a letter during their entire stay. So I asked myself, "How could we get people who are really interested in inmates to write them?" Out of this grew our FOAP (Friend of a Prisoner) program. A FOAP must agree to do four things: pray for the inmate daily; write him at least every thirty days; remember his birthday with a card or inexpensive gift; and remember the inmate at Christmas with a card or inexpensive gift. We started with the inmates who made commitments to Christ.

Right away, we ran into a problem. Some institutions have rules against gifts of any type. In these prisons, we ask that the FOAP's just send cards.

We are able to get hundreds of FOAP's during a city-wide crusade by simply telling about our program. Each person who agrees to be a FOAP receives a beautiful gold-plated medallion with the initials FOAP inscribed on it.

To date, we have several thousand people helping

to raise the morale of Christian inmates, telling them someone cares.

Invitations are coming in from all over the nation for crusades. I was talking the other day to Jerry Enomoto, the head of prisons for the state of California. I can remember when we first met him. At that time, he was warden at Tehachapi State Penitentiary near Bakersfield, California. It was our second prison crusade. It had been a great success. Enomoto said that he would like to keep in touch with us, and that he thought our work would continue to coincide. Sure enough, he's now head of prisons for the whole state of California. He wants us to visit the other institutions in his state. In addition, we have a blanket invitation from Governor Reuben Askew to visit all the other institutions in the state of Florida, and they're even talking about our going back to some of the ones we've already visited there. Most every state has expressed some interest in our prison ministry and we're trying to accommodate as many as possible.

We started out by doing two prison crusades a year; then it jumped to four, and then six. This past year, we conducted thirteen prison crusades.

I run into evidence of the Lord's blessing everywhere. The other night at a banquet in preparation for a city-wide crusade in Findlay, Ohio, a man came up to me after the banquet and said:

May I please have a moment of your time? You remember the Marion prison crusade? Well, one of the counselors from here in Findlay became deeply interested in an inmate there. He continually visited the inmate and when he would come back here to his home in Findlay, he told his family all about the man. The family grew interested in helping him. They were given a running account of his problems and victories.

After several months, the counselor became seriously ill. He died within a few weeks. Following the initial shock of her husband's death, the wife thought about the inmate that her husband had been so devoted to helping. The children continued to ask questions about the inmate. So, out of respect for her husband, she decided to go back and tell the inmate that her husband had died, and to reassure him of the continued prayers of the remaining members of the family.

The inmate invited her to visit him again. The woman thought it would please her husband, so she agreed. It became a weekly thing. Eventually, he proposed to her and upon his release, they were married. Today they have established a happy new family.

Such stories as this fill me with added enthusiasm for our work in prisons. How the Lord is using our people to turn things around for so many forgotten men.

One of the pluses of our prison crusades has been the blessings they have brought to our counselors. They have grown much in their spiritual lives, and of course, they have strengthened our ministry immeasurably.

There is a growing number of people who are becoming excited about the prison ministry, and who are stepping forward to help us. Not only is our entire prison ministry being run by four laymen, but there are hundreds of counselors who are almost as dedicated to its success.

Partly because of a post World War II increase in population and a renewed emphasis on punishment, there are more men and women in federal and state prisons today than any other time in the nation's history, according to an April, 1976 issue of the *Corrections Magazine*. At that time, there were 249,716 persons in prisons around the country. This is a ten percent increase over a year earlier. More than half of the prisoners are under thirty years of age. The increase is probably due to public opinion. The climate has shifted in favor of punishment, rather than rehabilitation.

I am not certain that any meaningful rehabilitation can be done in our prison system as it now stands. Unless we can somehow introduce the inmates in institutions to relationship with Christ, such that their lives are really changed, rehabilitation is ultimately impossible. There are authorities who would tell us that what we need are better work release programs, better facilities, more and better education, and some even claim that poor vitamin content in food causes crime. I would agree that these are all worthy, humane social goals, but even more pressing is the need to get the men and women in the institutions around this country to have a life-changing experience with the Lord. Over and over again, we've seen lives genuinely changed by new relationships to Christ.

Remember Billy Houchin? I recently got a letter from him written on Easter Sunday. His letter said:

> I thought that this day that our Lord arose would be just the perfect day to tell you that my heart, mind, soul and body belong to the one Love that I have been searching for all my life. I know that Christ sent you to Kentucky State Penitentiary so that I might receive him. I am still in my eight-by-six-foot cage, but Jesus is so very dear and near . . . I hope this finds you strong in our Lord. Give my best to your family. We had the Lord's supper here on the walk tonight. I have led two guys to the Lord in the last few weeks. They are struggling, but they are hungry for the One who satisfies all needs.

I have had an opportunity now to follow some of the inmates after the crusades and see them in their spiritual growth. Nick the Greek is now out of Mansfield State Reformatory, after four years, and is radiantly free, both physically and spiritually. He goes with us to all of our prison crusades, and works as a counselor and gives his testimony from the platform to the entire institution. He also stays in the prisons for at least a week after each crusade to help with the follow-up work. His adjustment to life on the outside is obviously complete and successful.

Mike Franklin is growing by leaps and bounds, though he is still in maximum security in Florida State Prison. Bill Houchin, as he says in his letter, is still in his eight-by-six-foot cell. Though bound physically, these men are free at last! They are changed people!

We plan to continue to go into institutions all over the country with our Total Person Weekend. We will introduce them to some of the great athletes in our nation, and some everyday folks, whom some may call squares. But they get to know them on a one-to-one basis. The athletes open doors. The counselors get to know and love the inmates and help with their spiritual needs. The follow-up demonstrates our continuing interest.

The counselors often become so involved with the inmates that they continue to work with them. Gene Kandels' experience is a case in point.

Gene has been with us all the way. He's a veterinarian and successful businessman. He became close to a black inmate from Marion who committed his life to Christ. The inmate began sharing his burning desire to go to college. Gene encouraged him, but he did more. When he got out of prison, Gene and his family took him into their home for over a year. The ex-con is making good grades in college and his other social contacts are commendable. Every barrier is being overcome. This is Christianity in action.

We are continuing to develop new and better techniques. In addition to doing three prison crusades at once in order to reach more inmates, we are also conducting them in connection with our city-wides, such as we did recently in Honolulu.

We brought special guests in for the city-wide and they remained in the Islands to help us conduct a prison crusade in the previously riot-torn Hawaii State Prison. The Lieutenant Governor, Nelson Doi, who is in charge of a task force to improve the prison system in Hawaii, became involved in our city-wide and in our prison crusade. I publicly said that the prison facilities in Hawaii were the worst I'd ever seen. I recently got a letter from the Lieutenant Governor, and he said:

> I just wanted to inform you that our legislature passed our $10.2 million appropriation request last night for the construction of a new statewide correctional facility. Since this was an administration request, I have no doubts that the governor will sign the measure. We hope to commence construction by summer, and have the facilities completed within two years. I wanted you to be among the first to know of this good news because of the tremendous ministry that you started here in our prison.

Though people have been aware of a great need for a prison in Hawaii for a long time, I am glad that I spoke up about the poor facilities there. Maybe our ministry at least prodded the legislature to act more quickly. At least ours was another small voice. But we are determined to have a big voice in helping inmates spiritually.

We also have become aware of the need to do crusades in women's prisons. Only about one in twenty inmates in the country are women, so naturally there is a smaller need there by sheer lack of numbers. However, we ventured into one of the largest women's prisons in the country when we visited Lowell Prison for Women in Florida. In April of 1976, we were in three prisons simultaneously in Florida—Lowell Prison for Men, Lowell for Women, and Sumter Prison, all located near Ocala.

Again, we took 150 counselors, but this time fifty of them were women. The fifty women counselors related beautifully to the women inmates. The female inmates were as interested in the clinics our athletes conducted as their counterparts. But especially for this occasion, we invited Madeline Manning Jackson, a gold medal winner in the 1972 Olympics. She is an exciting Christian who made a tremendous impact when she shared her testimony.

One of the really effective women counselors we took with us was Annette Joseph, wife of my good friend Tom. She called me several months ago saying, "You know, I really would like something new and exciting to do for the Lord. I love my husband and children and have a beautiful life. But I would just like a new challenge." I suggested that she go to Florida with us to the prison crusade for women. She worked in the prison in a wonderful way. She was bone tired after the crusade, but she was radiantly happy because she had been "shooting the tube" for the Lord in Florida.

Counselors are not only fulfilled, but are taught lessons in Christian love. J. T. Williams, who along with three other men have taken over the direction of the entire prison ministry, claims to have learned many things.

At the Federal Penitentiary in Lewisburg, Pennsylvania, I met a young black man who had tried many religions while searching for the truth. He was a bright young man, but very difficult to reach, and I shared with him on many occasions. Finally, during the Sunday morning testimony service, he made his profession of faith and asked Jesus to take control of his life. A while later, he wrote to me that I was the first white man who ever cared for him or seemed concerned about him, and that as we talked, my "color" faded away. In my own mind, I could understand the black color fading away, but I never considered that white would also fade.

I had much the same experience at LaGrange, Kentucky in 1974. I attended my first prison crusade. On the first afternoon, the second inmate I met was a twenty-four-year-old, who was known as "Hard Rock," and who had committed three murders in two states before he was seventeen years old, and had spent seven years in prison for those murders. His sentence was life plus fifty years. He was the runner-up Golden Gloves Champion for the state of Kentucky, and was the boxing champion of that prison. As I talked and shared with him almost an hour, I tried to find out many things about him. When it came time to go and eat, we walked together to the dining hall, which was about a block or two away from the recreation area. It dawned on me all of a sudden that I couldn't remember whether he was black or white, even though I had been talking to him on such a personal basis for over a hour. I then turned my head very quickly and saw that he was black. (That had *never* happened to me before.)

As I shared this experience with him, I told him the only explanation I could give was that Jesus loved us so much that he just takes the color away and makes us color blind.

As we continued to walk, I thought about the first inmate I'd met and remembered that he was black, also. That night, I prayed for that young black man from Tampa, Florida, that he would receive Christ. The next morning, one of the first people I saw was that inmate from Tampa. To my surprise, he was white and not black.

Obviously, our counselors cover the spectrum—theologically and politically. Some are conservative and some liberal. Some are educated. Some are uneducated. One counselor is a rock-ribbed conservative. He explained, "I'm against all this social action in our church." But he was anxious to help in our prison ministry. I was amazed to see him irate over the terrible food and crowded living conditions after one weekend at a state prison. "I'm going to write the governor," he fumed. I didn't explain that he was getting involved in social action.

When you begin to work with and get to know and love these people, it is unavoidable. How can you separate their spiritual needs from their social needs?

I remember a different counselor saying, "When I came to this prison, I was to the right of Herbert Hoover politically, but I had my eyes opened to some things!"

Again, J. T. Williams relates:

On the first evening of the prison crusade at the Lewisburg Federal Penitentiary, I was eating with an inmate and I noticed a rather "hot-shot" type of black man with tennis shoes and dark sun glasses, who kind of hopped over to the table and sat down next to me. He started riding me pretty hard, saying various things about do-gooders coming into the prison, but I was able to show him love instead of bitterness. After a while, he said, "Hey man, I shouldn't be jiving you, because you are doing what you think is right, and I think what you all are doing is a pretty good thing for all of us. Here you are giving us a good time, and in fact, I would be a Christian myself if I hadn't found something better." I told him that I had been a Christian for a long time and had been searching for a long, long time before to find the truth. For me Christianity was the greatest thing in the world. I told him if he knew something better, to please tell me about it. His reply was "money." Well, that took me back a little, because God has blessed me with money during most of my adult life, and while I had not shared that fact with anyone in any of the previous prison crusades, I knew God gives us opportunities at times. I told him I had made some money in my life, but had not found it better than Christianity. I said that either he knew something about money that I didn't, or I knew something about Christianity that he didn't.

He told me that he had made $10,000 to $15,000 per week for a whole year, and asked me if that wasn't a lot of money. I replied that it was a great deal of money, but that I had made over a million dollars in one year, but I hadn't found it that good. He said, "You mean you made over a million dollars in just one year?" I told him yes, but that wasn't the end of my story because even though I'd made more than that, at the same time, I lost well over two million dollars in the last year and a half. I didn't find making the money or losing it that significant, and it certainly did not take the place of Jesus in my life.

He said, "Man, losing that much money would just kill me; I couldn't ever get over it." I said, "Fellow, you have just answered my question. Jesus will never leave me, and yet money will leave us all. Money is a temporary thing, but the love of God never ceases, and once Jesus is inside of us, he is real—forever! So, I will take Christianity over money any day." I found later that this guy had made his money by robbing banks on a rather consistent basis, and had gained quite a bit of notoriety with the success he had achieved—until he got caught.

Four years ago when people tried to interest me in prison crusades, I tried to avoid the issue, hoping I could side-step it. I tried to say I was already overcommitted, that we didn't have enough financial support and that I wasn't the one to preach in prisons, but God answered every one of my reservations with a positive solution.

That's the way it is with God. One way or another he will get his way. Jonah, you'll recall, didn't like the idea of going to Ninevah. In fact, he hated the very thought of being God's representative to those heathens. Jonah was a coward with a capital C. So he tried to sail in the other direction, but it is just impossible to run from God. He sent a fierce storm and a great fish, but even a fish can't digest a backslidden minister. The whale got nauseated and vomitted him up. When he hit the beach, he took off running for Ninevah.

Well, I didn't resist that much, but I wasn't very excited about a prison ministry for our organization. I know it must have been nauseating to God, so he stirred up some others and no matter how hard I fought, the idea went forward. I even prayed that God would send someone else to those dark, musty holes. "Send someone who'd enjoy that kind of work," I prayed. Can you imagine such stupidity, such naïveté? Who would want to go?

Thank God, we don't always get our prayers answered the way we request, because if I had I would have missed the thrill of a lifetime. I gradually became aware that I'm on the firing line. I'm on the first team. I'm where the action is. I'm "shooting the tube!"

What's more, I'm going to keep right on going for broke, shooting the works, playing with abandon, because that is the way Christ wants it. When he says, "Follow me," you either have to drop your nets or keep fishing.

If God gets his hook in you, the more you fight the bloodier the water gets. And all the blood in the water is yours (he shed his only once). Struggle as much as you want, but you are hooked.

If you can't make up your mind, then you're still bound by the same chains that bind many of the inmates I meet behind bars. They are still held captive by the mistaken belief that the world holds something that God can't provide.

I'm committed to telling them and as many others who will listen to this worn-out football player that they are wrong. For only when you turn your life over to him will you be totally free.

That's the Good News I want to share with people on both sides of the iron bars.

1730